What the Top Small Group Movement Leaders Are Saying about *Planning Small Groups with Purpose*

"No single person or book has had more influence on my small group philosophy than Steve Gladen and his first book, *Small Groups with Purpose*. I am so thankful that Steve has now taken those concepts and given us a practical guide in *Planning Small Groups with Purpose* for implementing them in our ministries. This is a book that you and your team will return to over and over!"

Chris Surratt, small group and discipleship specialist, LifeWay Christian Resources; author of *Small Groups for the Rest of Us*

"If you've ever wanted to take a peek into how Saddleback plans for their successful small group ministry, this is your chance. Gladen sprinkles strategic questions throughout to help the small group point person think and plan for their own ministries based on their church culture. A really helpful resource!"

Amy Jackson, associate publisher of SmallGroups.com

"Small group leaders and those who support them are faced with a daunting task: how to find the wisdom to deal with problems that differ from group to group and leader to leader. What they wouldn't give to be at the elbow of a man who is in continual contact with hundreds of small group pastors as they bring their challenges and dilemmas to him! With this book, Steve Gladen, held by many to be the outstanding developer of small groups, invites you to see what he sees as group systems are put together and problems are resolved. For the beginner, he lays out a step-by-step approach. For the advanced leader, he gives a floor plan that allows immediate focusing on one or another aspect of a group's issues. No small group department should be without copies of this comprehensive and practical guide. This is the tool that can be shared with every level of leader in a small group system."

Carl George, author of *Nine Keys to Effective Small Group Leadership*

"This book provides an exceptionally useful, encouraging, and challenging combination of wisdom, visionary perspective, and lots of practical planning tools. These can help to nourish and develop small group leaders and quality programs, producing healthy, spiritually balanced, vitally focused small groups that are critically important in the life and ministry of any congregation. A much-needed planning and implementation resource for the serious leader in small group ministry."

Rev. Dr. Roberta Hestenes, teaching pastor, Bayside Church, California; former Fuller Seminary faculty member and president of Eastern University

"Do not just read this book. Work it. Implement, measure, assess. Question everything. Repeat. In *Planning Small Groups with Purpose*, Steve Gladen outlines a process for designing a group model and strategy that are uniquely fitted to your church. If you are just looking for easy answers, this is not the book for you. If you are looking for the right questions to lead you to the most relevant answers, then gather your team, open this book, and grab a pen. *Planning Small Groups with Purpose* isn't just a onetime read; it is a manual that will serve you for years to come."

Heather Zempel, discipleship pastor, National Community Church; author of *Community Is Messy* and *Amazed and Confused*

"I love Steve's work because it is always rooted in experience, forged in the crucible of real group life with dedicated leaders, and readily used or adapted in other churches. Mine this resource for all you can get!"

Dr. Bill Donahue, president of The LeaderSync Group; associate professor, Trinity Evangelical Divinity School

"This book is chock-full of both practical experience and deep insight. Steve Gladen has been leading small groups at Saddleback for twenty years. He knows what he's talking about. Yet he repeatedly exhorts the readers to follow principles, not models, and to understand their own cultural context. You'll find practical steps in each chapter to guide you along your small group journey. The section 'Saddleback's Top Ten Small Group Ministry Commitments' is worth the price of the book. Here's a taste: 'I will steer clear of the numbers game,' 'I will avoid the comparison trap,' and 'It is sinful to feel superior to another church or ministry.' Get ready to deepen your small group understanding as you read the pages of this very insightful book. Thanks, Steve, for sharing your years of practical, successful small group experience."

Joel Comiskey, PhD, president of Joel Comiskey Group, www.joelcomiskeygroup. com; author of *Groups That Thrive*

"Once again my friend Steve Gladen has provided another helpful resource for those of us in the trenches of group life. Reading and thoughtfully applying *Planning Small Groups with Purpose* to your local context might just be the most important things you'll do this year for your groups ministry."

Bill Willits, executive director of Ministry Environments, North Point Ministries; coauthor of *Creating Community*

"It has been many years since a book arrived that mixed small group foundations with a practical how-to guide. This book will walk you through important decisions as you build a groups ministry full of purpose. Steve is no mere philosopher of groups but a veteran with a proven track record for building one of the most life-changing small group ministries in modern times. If you are leading the charge of community, you must devour this book."

Bill Search, executive pastor of ministries, Crossings Community Church, Oklahoma City; author of *The Essential Guide for Small Group Leaders*

"This is an invaluable resource for all small group point people who want to propel their ministry to the next level. With insightful questions, biblical principles, practical ideas, and actionable content, Steve guides you through a meticulous process of defining, creating, planning, and developing a thriving small group ministry. This is a great tool to use with your ministry team to hone in on the vision, strategy, and tactics for growing a discipleship culture through healthy small groups in your church."

Carolyn Taketa, small groups pastor, Calvary Community Church

"Empowering the people of God to fulfill the great commandment and the Great Commission through small groups is by far the best way to achieve these two biblical mandates. In *Planning Small Groups with Purpose*, Steve provides a field-tested and practical implementation process that covers every aspect of launching and expanding healthy, missional groups. If your church, lead pastor, and you are ready to become the kind of church that makes disciples who in turn make disciples, this book's process is a great source of guidance."

Randall G. Neighbour, author of *The Naked Truth about Small Group Ministry*; president of TOUCH Outreach Ministries, Houston, Texas

"Steve once again offers an amazing resource for building small groups, all flowing from his three decades of experience. This book is not just a how-to manual; in true Steve form, it also gives thoughtful insights to assure that your small group model aligns with the heart and purpose of your church's overall ministry. No matter what small group model you have, this is a vital resource to help you assess what it takes to create, develop, and maintain life-changing groups in your context!"

Dave Enns, lead groups pastor, North Coast Church

"*Planning Small Groups with Purpose* presents the step-by-step process that has shaped small groups for many churches. This book provides a guide to plan for small groups, train leaders, and implement these groups in a congregation. I wholeheartedly recommend this book. I have seen it work."

Hamp Greene, associate pastor, Church of the Highlands, Birmingham, Alabama

"It is impossible for any of us to experience spiritual growth without trusted relationships in our lives, and small groups are the best place for each person in our churches to find those relationships. In *Planning Small Groups with Purpose*, Steve will show you how leveraging your church's unique culture and structure is the key to making your small groups thrive."

Jeff Galley, central LifeGroups and missions pastor, Life.Church

PLANNING
SMALL GROUPS
WITH
PURPOSE

PLANNING
SMALL GROUPS
WITH
PURPOSE

A FIELD-TESTED GUIDE TO DESIGN
AND GROW YOUR MINISTRY

STEVE GLADEN

BakerBooks

a division of Baker Publishing Group
Grand Rapids, Michigan

Published by Baker Books
a division of Baker Publishing Group
PO Box 6287, Grand Rapids, MI 49516-6287
www.bakerbooks.com

Printed in the United States of America

Library of Congress Cataloging-in-Publication Data
Names: Gladen, Steve, 1960– author.
Title: Planning small groups with purpose : a field-tested guide to design and grow your ministry / Steve Gladen.
Description: Grand Rapids : Baker Publishing Group, 2018.
Identifiers: LCCN 2017057380 | ISBN 9780801077890 (pbk.)
Subjects: LCSH: Church group work—Planning. | Small groups—Planning.
Classification: LCC BV652.2 .G4845 2018 | DDC 253/.7—dc23
LC record available at https://lccn.loc.gov/2017057380

18 19 20 21 22 23 24   7 6 5 4 3 2 1

In keeping with biblical principles of creation stewardship, Baker Publishing Group advocates the responsible use of our natural resources. As a member of the Green Press Initiative, our company uses recycled paper when possible. The text paper of this book is composed in part of post-consumer waste.

To the small group point persons,
my heroes,
who do not abdicate their responsibility
for leading the house-to-house movement.
Thanks for being willing to plan to succeed
versus just hoping it will happen.
You are critical to the kingdom.
Plan, press ahead, and persevere!

Contents

Acknowledgments

Many thanks to:

The senior pastors who have played a huge role in my life before Saddleback Church: Gene Speich, Paul Currie, George Smith, Charles Blair, Jason Garcia, and Larry DeWitt. Thanks for your role in shaping me for kingdom service.

Rick and Kay Warren, who have poured into me since 1983 without even knowing it. Your constant dedication to ministry, pastoral families, and the health of the church are overwhelming. You are the same in person as you are on the platform. Your sacrifice makes this book possible and the small group ministry of Saddleback Church what it is. I wish everyone could get a glimpse of the pastor I know day in and day out. You are my pastor. Thanks for leading!

Christi Hamilton, your passion for writing and making sense of my senseless thoughts has been the salvation for this book. You read my mind and brought this book to life! Christi, you and your family are a godsend to the Gladen family.

Brian Smith, editor extraordinaire. You encouraged, pushed, challenged, and made this book better! Thanks for all your time and passion and love for small groups.

Chad Allen, boy you put up with a lot from me! Thanks to you and Baker Publishing for believing in me and going on this journey . . . again!

Gina Rikimaru, who has lived this journey more than most by being next to me, making my ministry more effective for his kingdom. Your unseen hours devoted to Saddleback Church, the Small Group Team, and my family are appreciated more than you know.

The Small Group Pastors at all our campuses: Dave Alford, Aaron Amaya, Brandon Bathauer, Corrie Bowman, Larry Cherrison, Julie Chung, Laura Copeland, Jeff Feld, Eduardo Garcia, Jeff Gonzalez, Matt Graybill, Will Guzman, Ryan Hacker, Tom Kang, Jay Kranda, Karo Ku, Kevin Lee, Reagan Miura, Chris Reed, Glenn Reynolds, Aaron Roberts, Beth Schwartz, Brannon Shortt, John Simons, Jim Sonnenburg, Clay Stokes, Santosh Swamidass, Jason Williams, Jacob Wilson, Chris Yi, Sam Yoon, and Steve Yu.

The Small Group Network leadership: Eric Falcinella, Ron Wilbur, Gina Abbas, Jason Banzhoff, Brian Beall, Danny Bias, JT Black, Ryan Brammer, Philip Byers, Andrew Camp, Vinnie Cappetta, Tommy Carreras, Cynthia Considine, Steve Curran, Dennis Funk, Michael Grayston, Manie Groenewald, JW Hilliard, Mark Kendall, Nick Lenzi, Paul Lewis, Andrew Mason, Mark Mehlig, Jon Noto, Derek Olson, Greg Robins, Josh Rose, Carolyn Taketa, Kiersten Telzerow, Daniel Thomas, Dan Tupps, Tracey Ware, Joe Windham, Adam Workman, Matthew Wray, and Ron Youtsey, who make the SGN strong so we are better together!

Those who read the manuscript and gave suggestions that made this book better: Jason Williams, Carolyn Taketa, Barnaby and Alyssa Riedel, and Michael Gerber.

My small group, who has lived this crazy journey with Lisa and me: Dave and Molly Alford, Berto and Ruby Guzman, Todd and Tracy Jones, and Gina and Tyra Rikimaru. Our families are forever knit together.

My parents, Bill and Fern Gladen, who took a risk in their fifties to follow Christ and who are waiting for us in heaven—party on! To my brothers Kurt (in heaven), Greig, Todd (in heaven), Mark, and my brave sister Nita; I love life with you and wish geography wasn't between us. Thank the Lord for video calls!

Lisa, Erika, and Ethan, who I would die for and who are the reason I get up in the morning. Lisa, you cheer me on and give me grace, more than I deserve. Since 1988 you have believed in me and my ministry. You sacrifice more than anyone knows; you are an amazing mother and wife! I love you! Erika and Ethan, you bring a smile and a glimpse into the future. You are both turning into amazing young adults. I pray for your growth in the Lord, calling, and impact for his kingdom. Live strong for him!

To Jesus Christ who strengthens me and makes this whole work possible.

Foreword

When we first planted Saddleback Church, I understood that it wasn't about a physical structure. It was about transformed lives. People connected to God and each other, working together to minister to others in our community and around the world. And the one thing that has mobilized our congregation to step forward and meet need after need is our small group ministry.

In fact, Saddleback is an example of how just one small group can have a significant and powerful impact. When my wife, Kay, and I started the church, it was simply a small group that met in the living room of our rented apartment, and now forty years later, there are over 7,000 small groups within our congregation.

This has allowed us to grow larger as a congregation while also becoming smaller. How is that possible? Through the intimate fellowship in our small groups that connects people to each other at the heart level. We consistently have more people engaged in our small groups than attending our weekly worship services.

So much of this is due to the leadership of Steve Gladen, a pastor with a deep passion for Jesus and people. Steve has expanded and fine-tuned Saddleback's small group ministry for decades. He's learned what works, and he's learned what doesn't. That's valuable experience to tap into. And

Steve has generously shared what he's learned with thousands of church leaders who have started small group ministries.

The book you hold in your hands offers these same lessons from Steve, and I believe God can use it to radically change your small group ministry while creating greater intimacy among the people in your congregation. It will help increase outreach and service to your community and encourage small group members to work together to share the hope of Christ throughout the world.

Here's the thing. You may be overflowing with vision for your small group ministry, but there is a point where you have to stop thinking about it and talking about it and start doing something about it. There's a time to put your vision into action. I've met thousands of pastors with incredible vision for ministry, but sadly, they never got past the thinking stage. What good is a vision when it stays stuck in your head? Steve will take you past the thinking stage and show you how to take practical steps to turn your vision into faithful action.

I am convinced that small groups are the most effective way to harness the energy of millions of Christians. They equip and encourage believers to work together in order to fulfill the call of the Great Commission and the great commandment!

God bless you!

Rick Warren, Saddleback Church

Introduction

THE PURPOSE OF THIS BOOK

If you know anything about me, you know I love a plan. I have displayed on my office whiteboard, "Vision without implementation equals hallucination."[1] I believe in vision, and you'll hear me talk quite a bit about it in this book. If you don't have a plan for implementing your vision, you are wasting your time. After I wrote my first book, *Small Groups with Purpose*,[2] I discovered people still needed a step-by-step guide for planning their small group ministries, and that's the purpose of this book. If you read this book and complete its exercises, you will end up with a long-term plan, including specific twelve-month goals to start or accelerate your small group ministry.

Church culture is undeniably returning to small groups. And why not? The early church met to worship not only en masse but also in small groups, from house to house (see Acts 2:42–47). Thom S. Rainer published an article on May 10, 2017, titled, "Eight Major Changes in Churches the Past Ten Years." One of these changes:

Today: Vital importance of groups
Ten years ago: Marginal importance of groups

Healthy churches today make groups (community groups, home groups, Sunday school, life groups, etc.) a high priority. Ten years ago, many church leaders did not see how groups could enhance the health of the church in discipleship, evangelism, prayer, ministry, and fellowship.[3]

Success involves the management of ideas. Ideas can provide wonderful breakthroughs for your ministry. However, trying to implement too many ideas at once can crush or fragment your ministry.

In order to effectively manage and execute ideas in your context, you have to understand your church or ministry culture as well as the systems your church or ministry currently has in place. Not only will this book build on the concepts I wrote about in my book *Small Groups with Purpose*, but it will also help you grasp more deeply how to work within the culture and systems your church has in place. We will also investigate fresh, new ideas and processes that will move your ministry forward in an effective, efficient, and—most important—God-honoring way.

It is important to grasp that God never calls you merely to imitate another church's successful model. As I give you examples of what we do at Saddleback Church, I am not suggesting you do things exactly the same way. You know your church culture, and you know your ministry. So take the ideas we discuss and tailor them to your church environment. God has called you to *your* church, for *your* culture, in *your* location, for *this* time.

As you move through this book, you will be presented with a series of twenty planning questions, along with suggested practical answers, to help you develop a strategic plan. In my thirty-plus years of doing small group ministry, I have had to answer each of these questions, and you'll need to answer them too. I'm confident that if these questions haven't yet arisen in your ministry, they eventually will.

You'll come up with many answers to these questions as part of your plan, but you don't need to implement all of the answers at once. You do need to know what's ahead of you. This book will help shed light on the unknowns of small group ministry and help you plan efficiently and

> *God has called you to **your** church, for **your** culture, in **your** location, for **this** time.*

practically. I will even help you prioritize and calendarize your plan. I want you to succeed.

So no matter your denomination, church size, church paradigm, church polity, or church's location on this planet—if you will prayerfully, thoughtfully answer these questions, you will end up with a plan that will save you pain! (Smile.) Prayerfully approach each decision and idea, asking God to show you how it pertains to your ministry. Praying your way through this book will help you understand where the Lord is guiding your ministry.

Developing your ministry is not a linear process—step 1, then step 2, then step 3. Since this process is multidimensional and the order of your actions is unpredictable, I have structured the book around the metaphorical motif of building a home (which is kind of fitting, since most small groups meet in homes—but definitely don't have to!). A sound, secure home needs a strong foundation, so part 1 focuses on the foundation of your ministry. This prevents you from building your house on the sand, so it won't crumble when trouble comes (see Luke 6:46–49).

After that, in part 2 we will walk through five areas of the home, exploring four planning questions in each area:

1. The kitchen, where people *connect*
2. The family room, where people *grow*
3. The study, where people *invest*
4. The front door, where people *reach* others
5. The dining room, where family *sustains*

Each area, with its cluster of four questions, emphasizes a different aspect of your ministry, each critical to complete and necessary for long-term effectiveness. Even though this book progresses from one area to the next, the actual implementation of your plan will involve roaming back and forth among different areas. Stay flexible, and discover all that is in your home.

Feel free to use this book with flexibility. It is a dynamic, working document that you can refer back to as you grow your ministry. Take notes, write in the margins, highlight—whatever works best for you.

In this book, you will learn from Saddleback campuses of varying sizes that have developed small group ministries. You will also read testimonies from people who have attended our Accelerate! conference, which focuses on building small group ministries. These attendees come from different size churches, different denominations, and different cultures. Their encouraging feedback is my motivation for writing this book.

For example, I received this email from James Whitely, small group pastor from Word of Faith Family Worship Cathedral in Austell, Georgia:

> My goal was to gain a better understanding of how to shape our church's small group ministry. Our church is a large, predominantly African American congregation, and there are not many effective models of authentic and effective small group ministries to research. So I attended the Accelerate! conference to start this journey, building a life-changing small group ministry in our specific church demographic.
>
> I have studied several of the successful Caucasian megachurches, but I wanted a hands-on approach to building and organizing a small group ministry from the ground up. After returning from the conference to my church in Atlanta, we launched our small group ministry in January 2017 with fifty-one adult groups that engage over five hundred of our members. To God be the glory!
>
> Your guidance helped me focus in on the main things, and then begin applying the principles to help build a thriving, authentic, and loving small group ministry at our church.

My prayer is that you, too, walk away empowered with a new arsenal of strategies and tools for starting your small group ministry or reenergizing the growth, influence, and reach of your existing ministry.

PART I

The Foundation

1

Think Churchwide

Each local church is meant to be a unified body, working together in a coordinated way toward a common purpose. That means, as you plan your small group ministry, you should start by thinking churchwide. The weekend services, the small groups, and the other church ministries all work together to achieve the outcome of a mature disciple—what Saddleback calls the Purpose Driven Life.

Whole-church coordination doesn't happen by accident. It takes intentionality. As Christians it is possible to get caught in the passive "If God wants it to happen, it will happen" trap, and this can often lead to . . . absolutely nothing. While it's true that the Lord can and does make things happen, he has also equipped us to be his hands and feet. Therefore, the best kingdom outcomes require that we become intentional in our planning while depending continually on the Lord for wisdom.

Define Your Church's Success, System, and Plan

The coordinated functioning of your local body requires understanding clearly what *success* means for your church. What is God's end for your church that you must keep in view? This is defined in your church's and your small group ministry's vision and mission statements, which we will discuss in chapter 4.

Based on this definition of success, it is imperative to have a churchwide *system* that moves people along a comprehensive pathway toward the end destination of mature disciples. Without such a unified system, a new or existing ministry, like small groups, will follow its own independent path, which may not take people along the pathway to success for your church. You may end up with chaos resembling that of the Tower of Babel. Your church's leadership must prayerfully communicate and work together to create a roadmap for your church that will help both leaders and congregants fulfill the church's vision and mission, guiding everyone toward eternal success. This chapter (and parts of chapters 4 and 5) discusses these whole-church considerations.

Within the whole-church system, each ministry—including your small group ministry—must develop a comprehensive *plan* that fits within the system and helps achieve your church's vision and mission. This is your ministry's pathway to help achieve God's end purpose for your church, and most of this book will help you develop that ministry plan. Average small group pastors provide training. Good small group pastors have a plan encompassing only their ministry. Great small group pastors have a plan that is coordinated with the church's vision and mission.

Let's consider your churchwide system. You may already have a good system in place, or maybe your church leaders need to continue working to create or refine your system. In the rest of this chapter I will share some principles to help guide this process, illustrating these principles by describing how we accomplish them at Saddleback Church.

Everything we do at Saddleback is based on two passages of Scripture: Jesus's Great Commission (Matt. 28:19–20) and his great commandment (Matt. 22:37–40). Our senior pastor, Rick Warren, sums up our philosophy in *The Purpose Driven Church*: "These two passages summarize everything we do at Saddleback Church. If an activity or program fulfills one of these commands, we do it. If it doesn't, we don't."[1]

In these two passages we find five biblical purposes:

> *Great small group pastors have a plan that is coordinated with the church's vision and mission.*

Fellowship: "Baptizing them in the name of the Father and of the Son and of the Holy Spirit" (28:19).

Discipleship: "Teaching them to obey everything I have commanded you" (28:20).

Ministry: "Love your neighbor as yourself" (22:39).

Evangelism: "Go and make disciples of all nations" (28:19).

Worship: "Love the Lord your God with all your heart and with all your soul and with all your mind" (22:37).

Our small group philosophy reflects the philosophy of the overall church. It is not enough for us to think about these purposes in the corporate structure of the church alone. It is not enough for people to be exposed to the five purposes only on weekends. We want them to experience the five biblical purposes in the context of a small group so that ultimately they become part of daily life, a purpose driven life.

Small groups were foundational to the early church, but what did they do? The answer includes all five of these biblical purposes, as shown in Acts 2:42–47:

> They devoted themselves to the apostles' teaching and to fellowship, to the breaking of bread and to prayer. Everyone was filled with awe at the many wonders and signs performed by the apostles. All the believers were together and had everything in common. They sold property and possessions to give to anyone who had need. Every day they continued to meet together in the temple courts. They broke bread in their homes and ate together with glad and sincere hearts, praising God and enjoying the favor of all the people. And the Lord added to their number daily those who were being saved.

The small groups described in Acts that met in homes were a strategic part of the greater church, and it is particularly significant that they *balanced* the biblical purposes, which is the basis for spiritual health. As was true in biblical times, this balance of the purposes is vital to the health of small groups today.

Unfortunately, today many small groups focus on one purpose only. A group may be a fellowship group, a service group, a discipleship group, or some other kind of group. At Saddleback we found that if we wanted discipleship to happen, we had to instill the idea of balance into the DNA of the church, into every small group of the church, and into every individual life in the church.

1. They Fellowshiped

Membership in the body of Christ means we can identify with a family—God's family. "They devoted themselves . . . to fellowship . . . and ate together with glad and sincere hearts" (Acts 2:42, 46). It has always interested me that right after Jesus was baptized and then tempted in the desert, one of the first things he did was get twelve guys and form a small group. Even Jesus saw the value of relational discipleship in a group context and the need for fellowship and authenticity.

2. They Were Discipled and Grew Spiritually

The Bible says, "They devoted themselves to the apostles' teaching" (Acts 2:42). That means they devoted themselves to growing in Christ and maturity. Evidently not only did they listen to what the apostles were teaching in the temple courts on the Sabbath and other days, but these people also gathered in their homes and studied and practiced what was being taught in the temple courts.

3. They Ministered to Each Other

"They sold property and possessions to give to anyone who had need" (Acts 2:45). That's ministry—believer to believer. These groups became an outlet for support, ministry, benevolence, charity, and sharing meals.

4. They Evangelized the Lost

This was their mission: "The Lord added to their number daily those who were being saved" (Acts 2:47). If you only go fishing once a week—a fishing service—you are only going to catch fish then. If you go fishing throughout the week—through small groups—the number of fish will increase dramatically. When all five biblical purposes are happening within your groups and in the lives of each group member, the natural by-product is evangelism. People are attracted to the kind of changes they see in the lives of healthy Christians.

5. *They Worshiped*

"They devoted themselves . . . to the breaking of bread and to prayer. . . . [They were] praising God" (2:42, 47). In other words, these early Christians worshiped in their homes. And what was the result? "Everyone was filled with awe at the many wonders and signs performed by the apostles" (2:43). The bottom line is that God shows up when people make room for him.

Learning the Difference between a Ministry and a Small Group

In his book *The Purpose Driven Church*, Rick Warren wrote, "We don't expect each small group to do the same things; we allow them to specialize."[2] That was in 1995. As time went by, we began to learn more about two types of groups at Saddleback: "balanced" small groups and specialty groups that predominantly focus on one purpose.

Specialty groups that meet around special interests or ministries are strategic, but their goal is not to balance the five biblical purposes (fellowship, discipleship, ministry, evangelism, and worship) to create healthy individuals and groups. For example, while our greeters ministry groups are an important and strategic ministry of the church, those groups don't generally focus on the *health* of the individuals and group but instead on greeting people who come to our campus. All of our specialty groups (ministries) overemphasize one of the purposes. In this example of greeters, it overemphasizes ministry. I could give hundreds of examples of ministries in each of the five biblical purposes (see pages 31–32).

Our balanced small groups, on the other hand, focus on individual and group health through all five biblical purposes. We are far more concerned about *healthy* groups than we are about the *number* of small groups. Having many groups or even having a large percentage of our people in groups is not the ultimate goal because it is possible to have a large number of small groups that are not producing fruit or life change.

At Saddleback we still have specialty groups that don't balance all five purposes, and they are important. (Most churches call them ministries.) But we expect all other small groups to focus on health through balancing all five biblical purposes. And we encourage each member of a specialty group also to participate in a balanced small group for the sake of his or her spiritual health. This book's focus is on developing balanced small groups in your church.

Church Systems for Growth

The entire structure of Saddleback Church's vision and mission is based on two settings for gathering, growing, ministering, evangelizing, and worshiping as believers, drawn from Acts 5:42: "Day after day, in the temple courts and from house to house, they never stopped teaching and proclaiming the good news that Jesus is the Messiah." In fact, the normative church structure throughout the New Testament included temple courts and house-to-house gatherings. This book will focus on the house-to-house side, but we will keep in view the larger picture of the goal of getting people to a weekend service and then to a place where God is daily using them in their giftedness (carried out in a specialty group). This will help you build a strategic plan for an effective small group ministry merged purposefully into the culture and context of your churchwide system.

Figure 1.1 represents Saddleback's churchwide system—our environment—and it may be similar to your church's environment. It represents three doors by which someone may enter—the main worship center, the small group ministry, and the other church ministries, which are specialty groups. It doesn't matter which door someone uses to enter your church; it only matters that they get there and end up working together for the advancement of God's kingdom. None of these three is more important than the others.

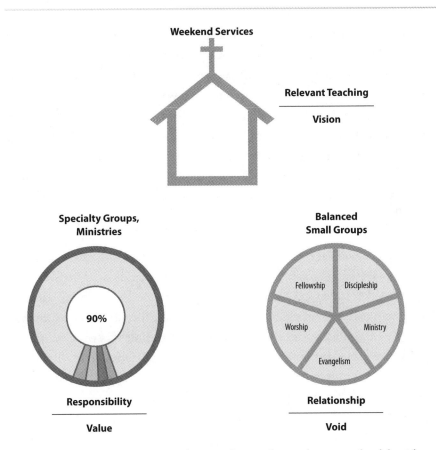

Figure 1.1

Your body has nine systems that work together to keep you healthy (the skeletal system, the circulatory system, and so on). When one of those systems isn't healthy, your body is in dis-ease, from which we derive the word *disease*. Similarly your church's three systems must all be healthy and remain in harmony with each other.

Motivate People by Addressing Felt Needs

In God's providence these three church systems correspond with three significant felt needs of people—*relevance*, *relationship*, and *responsibility*. Addressing people's felt needs through the church environment is essential for keeping people motivated and involved.

Motivating people is one of the biggest challenges for most churches. Each person has 168 hours per week, and each one is understandably selective about how to distribute those hours among the many possible uses. How many times have you asked people to spend time in a church activity and heard the response, "I'm too busy"? You can empathize because you also struggle with priorities for your limited time. In some respects this response is legitimate because people are busy. But it's often a handy excuse to get out of a commitment people simply aren't motivated about. They don't perceive that their choices about how to use their time are likely based on fulfilling a need about which they feel strongly. But if people discover that the activities you present in your church environment *do* meet their felt needs, they will eagerly commit part of their 168 hours to those activities.

People's first major felt need, relevance, is best addressed in the temple courts—that is, in weekend services—through relevant teaching. The Pew Forum, a research center on religion and public life, studied reasons why people choose a church. The number one criterion was the quality and relevance of the sermons. So when Rick, during his series on the Ten Commandments, taught on "You shall not commit adultery" (Exod. 20:14), he titled his sermon, "How to Affair-Proof Your Marriage." He taught straight from Scripture while making the topic relevant to today's marriages. Some pastors, when they make their teaching relevant to people's lives, are criticized for "watering down" their sermons. But people only attend and listen and change when we teach solid biblical truth in a way that is practical and applicable to them. Relevant teaching doesn't require compromising God's Word, and it meets people's felt needs and real needs by addressing the issues they face each day. Relevant teaching inspires people to move from passively sitting and listening to active growth and commitment to their church.

The second great felt need of people is relationship—vertically with the Lord and horizontally with people—and it is best addressed in small groups that are balanced in addressing the five biblical purposes (fellowship, discipleship, ministry, evangelism, and worship). They accomplish everything encompassed in Jesus's Great Commission and great commandment.

Even the biggest loner naturally craves connection. Your whole church environment—and especially your small groups—will motivate people to invest their time by fully addressing their need for relational connection.

Once people understand their purpose and why they were created (for the vertical relationship with God), and they learn how to flesh that out relationally (in the horizontal relationships with people) by interfacing with this broken world, they will understand how God wants biblical fellowship to happen. When relationship moves from below the surface to authenticity, it takes on new meaning.

Third, people love to feel needed, to possess some level of *responsibility*. This need draws people to opportunities in your varied church ministries. These are specialty groups that emphasize one of the five biblical purposes (from Jesus's Great Commission and great commandment) over the others.

- *Fellowship*. These groups love fellowship and tend to be great assimilation engines for the church. Examples include scrapbooking, knitting, sports, and adventure groups.
- *Discipleship*. These groups love learning and strengthen the church's cognitive growth. Examples include classes that teach theology, skills, and spiritual practices.
- *Ministry*. These groups generally fall into two buckets—task groups and caring groups. Examples of task groups include ushers, parking, greeting, landscaping, and cleaning teams. Examples of care groups include support, recovery, and counseling groups.
- *Evangelism*. These groups love putting the gospel into action. Examples include local outreach groups impacting the community, teams for global trips impacting the world, and centers that meet needs, such as Saddleback's PEACE Center, which provides food, education, and medical care.
- *Worship*. These groups care about worship and the fine arts. Examples include worship groups, choirs, and people who enjoy the

arts, such as painting. Art is a powerful medium in culture around our campuses and in local art galleries. For the five hundredth anniversary celebration of the Reformation, we did huge paintings of each of the five solas.

When responsibility changes from a chore to a passion, people feel valued.

Though these specialty groups don't address all of the biblical purposes, the plus side is that members have responsibility and are contributing, so they feel more a part of the church. And once people become active contributors together, their bonds with each other grow exponentially. When responsibility changes from a chore to a passion, people feel valued.

So how does your church move from just motivating people to making them long-term, engaged members of your church? Let me focus on three V words that correspond to each felt need: *vision, void,* and *value.*

First, relevant teaching not only brings people into the church but also makes them stay by providing a *vision* that is bigger than the individual and in which the person can believe. Second, small groups help people get below the surface, filling the spiritual *void* with knowledge of the Creator and in belonging with each other. Third, through active ministry people find *value* by contributing where God has gifted them as an active part of the church.

These three felt needs are your church's targets, and you should work hard to hit them. Don't lower your expectations or requirements when people say they're too busy; rather, work harder at running your programs to address felt needs so that people will be drawn in and want to stay and participate. Time is not the issue; the issue is how the church answers felt needs. When you provide ways to address people's needs for relevance, relationship, and responsibility, they will give you time from their 168 hours!

Don't say no for people. When you meet their felt need, they will say *yes!* Then watch with amazement the fresh energy and renewal that fills your church. How do I know this works? I have seen it happen at Saddleback Church, where the busiest people make time for things that matter. "Behold, I am doing a new thing; now it springs forth, do you not perceive it? I will make a way in the wilderness and rivers in the desert" (Isa. 43:19 ESV).

Test Case: Saddleback's Churchwide Plan

Let me now overview Saddleback's whole-church plan—one of many ways to put all of these pieces together as a pathway for guiding people toward maturity and powerful service. This plan can be represented by a funnel (see figure 1.2). What does a funnel do? Its wide end gathers widely scattered items and draws them toward the narrow end.

Saddleback's funnel invites people to interesting, low-commitment activities and starts them down a pathway toward narrowly focused maturity and high commitment. At Saddleback Church we fulfill the Great Commission and the great commandment through our funnel. You will need to establish your own pathway for people and determine what you want to accomplish as people move along your pathway. As you read, think of this like eating fish: eat the meat and throw away the bones. Choose what works for you and leave what doesn't. Derive from this what works for your ministry, in your church.

Our desire is to see the Great Commission and great commandment burned into our people's hearts and lived out on a daily basis. Following are brief descriptions of the four main "spaces" a person moves through

> *Time is not the issue; the issue is how the church answers felt needs.*

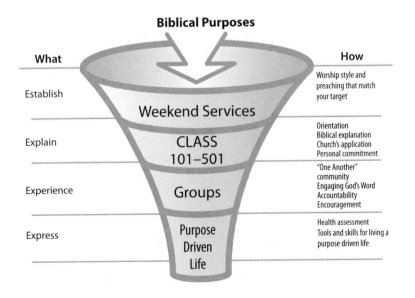

Figure 1.2

in Saddleback's funnel—through four types of encounters: *establish*, *explain*, *experience*, and *express*.

Weekend Services

This is the entry point for most people, where they begin to discover what our church is about. This is where we *establish* our paradigm through preaching, teaching, and testimonies. This is the best opportunity to promote the rest of our funnel, our pathway for people.

CLASS

At Saddleback we have a series of four Christian Life and Service Seminars (CLASSes) to help people understand themselves, God's plan for them, and our church's various learning and ministry opportunities. In these we *explain* in depth the critical steps by which Jesus's followers can fulfill his Great Commission and his great commandment. Remember, you must build something that works for your church. Be creative, and don't be afraid to color outside the lines to build the best program for your church. But understand the sequence, as outlined below. People need to commit to a church, they need habits to last in their Christian walk, they need to contribute, and they must reach out.

CLASS 101 is designed to introduce the fundamentals of why our church exists—our structure, our systems, our story, our salvation. This is our *membership* class, which explains how one belongs in our family. People sometimes ask how important church membership is. We believe it is vitally important, just as marriage is important as the alternative to living together. We all recognize the value of standing up and making a public declaration. We become what we are committed to; this class inspires deeper commitment.

CLASS 201 goes deeper in *maturity* and explains how to slay the common Orange County giants of busyness, materialism, and isolation, through which the devil loves to operate. We present the Bible's answers for developing healthy habits—regular time with God, tithing, and relational connection to the church community, especially through small groups.

In CLASS 301 we help our church members discover their unique God-given design and get involved in a *ministry*. We call this their **SHAPE**:

S—*Spiritual gifts.* What has God supernaturally gifted me to do?

H—*Heart.* What do I have a passion for and love to do?

A—*Abilities.* What natural talents do I have?

P—*Personality.* Where does my personality best suit me to serve?

E—*Experiences.* How have my spiritual, painful, educational, and ministry experiences prepared me for service?

Then in CLASS 401 we teach about personal, local, and global evangelism—our *mission* step. We are not spectators in this world; we are the hands and feet of Jesus. So we want our members actively evangelizing in fields near and far. We call our mission the PEACE Plan, about which you can learn more at www.ThePeacePlan.com.

We are currently experimenting with CLASS 501, in which we dig deep into surrender and sacrifice to *magnify* the Lord, growing closer to him. We may do this through small group retreats.

Small Groups

The next level down our funnel is small groups—the central purpose of this book. This is the context where people start to *experience* true spiritual formation. It's the best place for people to fulfill the house-to-house aspects of Jesus's Great Commission and great commandment (see Acts 2:42–47). Small groups are where people get real, going beyond the safe public persona we allow most people to see. It's only in deeper relationships that we realize healing for our pain and our potential for impact according to God's purpose.

Saddleback offers three types of balanced small groups, all of which aim toward the same outcome: balancing Jesus's Great Commission and great commandment in the heart of each person and group. The strategies are a bit different, and we've brought them to various stages of development—*crawl* (we're starting to figure it out), *walk* (we're well on our way), and *run* (well developed, with room for improvement).

Traditional groups are at the *run* level. These meet any time of the week, both on the church campus and elsewhere. Most off-campus groups meet in homes, but others meet in coffee shops, parks, yachts (personally, I like these), and trains. We even have a group that meets at 35,000 feet—flight attendants meeting during long flights. These traditional groups generally meet weekly for about two hours. For more information on these groups, see *Leading Small Groups with Purpose*.

Workplace groups are at the *crawl* level. They target the same outcome, but we have discovered the hard way that a traditional group strategy doesn't always play out in the workforce. Our three hundred workplace groups (2 percent of our congregation's involvement) are largely evangelistic, and we are now employing a five-step strategy to draw in unbelieving coworkers:

W—Wear your faith (on clothes, pens, coffee cups) to discover interest in others.

O—Online resources provide biblical answers to questions.

R—Reach colleagues through "planting and watering" opportunities (see 1 Cor. 3:6).

K—Kindle community through a study that paves the way to a workplace group.

S—Strengthen each other in a workplace group.

For more information, email workplace@saddleback.com.

Virtual groups are at the *walk* development stage and meet in an online environment. Their strategy: "Meet people where they are, bring them where we want," using a six-step process described below. Online groups also serve to launch new campuses, called Saddleback Anywhere.

1. *Community.* We invite people to watch our online service at www .saddleback.com/online. We've found that these people stay engaged

in the life of the church, and new people can check out church before stepping through the door. Your website or online service *is* your first-impression ministry. When baseball was first televised, many said that people would stop coming to the ballparks. But the opposite happened. Make the most of your gold mine of possibilities through your online presence.

2. *Crowd.* You can visit our website to see the varied ways we engage online attendees. At the time of this writing, 4,411 people have reported accepting Christ through our online service. Thousands have engaged in other ways.

3. *Congregation.* People can start or join virtual small groups based on time zones. We have over 1,800 online groups. But we don't want to leave them there!

4. *Committed.* We encourage people to start a local small group with two or more friends. We have helped 63 percent of our online groups step away from the safety of the virtual environment and start meeting with people in person.

5. *Core.* Some local small groups gather to watch our weekend services together in addition to their small group meetings.

6. *Commissioned.* Some clusters of small groups or individuals in a local area gather monthly, which then becomes weekly, to start a Saddleback Anywhere campus.

For more information, email online@saddleback.com.

Purpose Driven Life

At the narrow end of the funnel is Purpose Driven Life, where people learn to actively *express* their faith and growth through action. These people have etched the Great Commission and the great commandment on their hearts. This is the narrowest part of the funnel, not because few people belong here—we *all* belong here—but because few people rise to this level of commitment. A mature and vibrant church sees a higher-than-normal fraction of its members live at this level, but this fraction may still be less than half, especially if the church is attracting new and young believers through the wide end of the funnel. At this stage of their journey, people carefully evaluate and plan their progress toward the five biblical purposes:

- *Fellowship*, engaging with God, family, and small group
- *Discipleship*, taking the next steps in spiritual formation
- *Ministry*, advancing God's kingdom through volunteer opportunities, held accountable to exercise our spiritual gifts in service
- *Evangelism*, sharing on personal, local, and global levels, all of which we greatly emphasize at Saddleback
- *Worship*, evaluating one's surrender and life as a living sacrifice to our King

Temple Courts and House to House

Figure 1.3 illustrates the two types of settings in which people progress along the growth pathway. Above the middle line are the steps that take place in the temple courts. These activities, such as the weekend service and CLASS, involve *presentation*, in which people sit in rows and listen to teaching.

Below the line are the pathway stages that take place house to house, involving more conversation and interaction, with emphasis on relationships. People are more likely to sit in a circle, as in small groups.

Everything above the line tends to be about knowledge, and below the line is more about application. Above the line is about information, while below the line is about transformation. This is how Saddleback ensures that the temple courts and house-to-house elements complement each other. People absorb knowledge with their heads (above the line), and then embed it in their hearts and lives (below the line) in relational community.

Your people need both solid biblical teaching and relational environments in which to apply what they're learning. And small groups play a critical role in strengthening relationships. If you're not seeing disciples

Figure 1.3

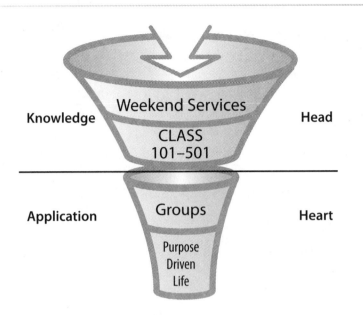

being made, or people aren't challenging themselves spiritually, or you're having trouble finding volunteers, check the relational temperature of your community. Also, as the relationships within your church strengthen, you will see people actively bringing others to church, and you will see surrender and sacrifice happen in ways you have never seen before. In John 13:34–35, Jesus said that our witness and attractiveness to others is based on our love for each other, within the church.

At Saddleback we seek to optimize the genius of God's design for the church through the complementary settings of temple courts and house to house, building both truthful knowledge and deep relationships for growth and impact.

Control or Growth?

One more concept to consider as you think churchwide is as Pastor Rick says, "You can structure either for growth or for control." It is impossible to structure for both. Churches that structure for high control tend not to see high growth. I love this!

We prefer church to be more like a hospital than a hotel. Hotels are neat and tidy, but in an emergency room you may see chaos and messiness—yet it is a place of healing. Sick people enter the doors of your church, and hopefully they at least begin the healing process while they're there. In the New Testament Epistles we see messy, chaotic churches, but miraculously they survived, and the corporate church has survived for two thousand years. That's because the Holy Spirit works even in messy imperfection to create places of God-centered healing.

We think it's okay to feel out of control if the result is growth. We prefer to release the reins a bit and leave a lot of the control to the Holy Spirit. That means refusing to let "problem solving" stop or hinder us when we could move ahead under God's direction. It can get messy, but fear not!

Let me give you an example. You may know how Saddleback Church came to possess the Rancho Capistrano property during the early 2000s. Years earlier we looked into buying the property, but we just couldn't swing it financially. God's delays are not God's denials. A number of years later, the church that owned the property was facing bankruptcy, which opened a new door for us. But the property cost was still high.

You can structure either for growth or for control.

At that time we had a few established campuses, but we didn't plan a new campus at this site. We wanted the property for its conference retreat center, where we hoped to train pastors. The Oklahoma City company Hobby Lobby, known for its generous support for Christian nonprofits, ended up buying the property, then came to us a year later and said, "We are going to donate this property to you." Donate! They paid over $22 million for the land and just gave it to us. Well, actually they rented the property to us for one dollar per month for a year. Then they gave it to us. As a bonus, we discovered the property also had a chapel, something for which we had been praying.

Simple, right? No. Sometimes when you receive something free, it comes with unforeseen costs. Some of the facilities had suffered from four to seven years of disuse and needed extensive repairs before we could use them. The prospect looked bleak.

But during a management meeting Rick said, "I don't want to worry about problem solving right now."

What? Problem solving seemed the next logical step. But Rick was asking us not to presume that all the solutions were in our hands alone. If God had given us the property, we needed to pray for his solutions to the problems. And in fact, in that first year three miracles happened.

The first was the tens of thousands of volunteer hours with which we were blessed. The donated work was invaluable. To this day we only have one full-time person who manages the 170-acre property. All the rest of the work is done by volunteers.

Second, a Saddleback member told us the Lord had put it on his heart to replace all the roofs. Third, another person matched every air-conditioning unit we bought.

All of this led to another, totally unexpected, fourth miracle: This site has become one of Saddleback Church's twenty campuses and now serves 1,500 people every weekend at its four services.

Release the messiness to God. He has a plan. You will notice as you read the New Testament that two-thirds of it is written about how messy the church is. Shake off any lingering self-righteousness and understand that you must be praying and thinking about how you are going to structure your church for a healthy small group ministry.

Manage Change with Love and Patience

Understanding must come before implementation. As the structure of your ministry begins to coalesce, you need to understand the goals of key leaders, especially senior leadership. You need to understand your church's culture and small group history. And watch carefully for the issues over which people—especially leaders—may be unpredictably sensitive. Change is always hard and often meets with fear and resistance, even if the change is right.

Even if you have been at your church for quite a while, make sure you review the church's history with leaders and ask clarifying questions over a meal or coffee. Understand the past so you can shape the future. Always listen carefully and seek to understand before you try to be understood. This will help you measure people's trust in your leadership. You want to have a firm grip on these things before you attempt to implement any new ministry or ideas. It is detrimental to the overall health of your church if your ministry is not completely aligned with the church as a whole or with other church ministries.

First, you need to interview key opinion leaders in your church. Get to know them. Listen, listen, listen. Determining their goals helps you strategize and execute your plan in an efficient and effective manner, leading to churchwide alignment.

Second, survey current small group leaders and adult Sunday school teachers about their past experience. What have they been doing? How have they been supported by the church's leaders? What makes for a successful community in their minds?

From the stories you hear, try to discern: Has the church history been positive? Are new concepts embraced or resisted? Has trust been broken? By what? The answers tell you a lot about where you can go and how fast you will get there. You can also uncover hidden land mines—actions or statements that may trigger negative reactions in others.

Understand the past so you can shape the future.

It's good to ask, "How would you go about making changes in this church?" The answer may give you a wise roadmap for your efforts.

Take your time. This process doesn't happen quickly. By taking adequate time early, you will save tons of time on the back side of implementation. These conversations *will* happen! It is your call whether you want to have them before you implement change, using a relational approach, or after, as you repair damaged relationships and trust.

By doing all of this with care you will honor the past in a way that will help you progressively move into the future. Pray for the responsiveness of your church. Pray for leaders the Lord will raise up. Pray about timing. And pray for what the Lord wants you to accomplish.

Take a few minutes and respond thoughtfully to the following three questions:

Which people or ministries in your church are open and responsive to considering changes?

What concerns do people have to which you need to be sensitive?

With whom should you have follow-up conversations? When? Who is thinking it over but not yet on board? Who is actively resistant?

Your answers will help determine the ease or difficulty of your path ahead. When starting a small group ministry, you are eager to see the fruit of your labor. But building before the foundation is ready *always* proves unwise. Trust me, I've done it both ways. Do it right the first time.

As much as we like to believe we are immune to statistics and numbers, some are inarguable. Whenever a new idea is introduced, acceptance of change runs pretty true to the Rogers Diffusion of Innovation Bell Curve (see figure 1.4). You will typically encounter about 16 percent eager early adopters, 34 percent early mid-adopters, 34 percent late mid-adopters, and 16 percent resistant late adopters. In light of this time-proven reality, don't be discouraged if your good ideas don't garner overwhelming support. With patience and wisdom, you will ultimately see wide adoption,

Figure 1.4

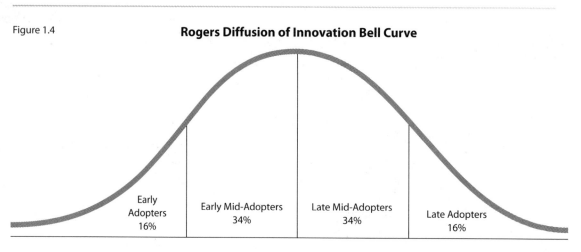

Rogers Diffusion of Innovation Bell Curve

Early
Adopters
16%

Early Mid-Adopters
34%

Late Mid-Adopters
34%

Late Adopters
16%

so stay the course. Meanwhile, focus most of your energy at first on those who see your vision from the start, and make them your allies in helping others see it.

We will come back to the importance of working in unity with church and ministry leadership in chapters 4 and 5.

2

Lead as a Team

As your plans coalesce, keep reminding yourself that *you are better together*. Maybe you have heard the adage, "If you want to move fast, go alone. If you want to move far, go together." Don't build this plan in isolation! Build on your strengths and strengthen your weaknesses through the strengths of others. Many leaders naturally tend to think they can do it better and faster alone. But no one person will think of everything. You need others. Embrace people to help better you; don't just assume more people will merely get in your way.

Who can you pull into your teams? Who can you challenge to help make an eternal difference in your church? Who will help you accomplish cultural change? Who will help you launch your ministry plan?

What teams and players will you need? Let me overview a few of the key parts most small group ministries need, especially as they grow.

Small Group Leaders

Small group leaders are the bedrock of any size ministry because they are your frontline leaders. As I will explain later, at Saddleback we call them *Hosts*. We take all who are willing to form groups with two or more

Build on your strengths and strengthen your weaknesses through the strengths of others.

friends, and we develop them into Christ followers who reflect Jesus's Great Commission and great commandment in their hearts and in the hearts of others. We train Hosts to help all group members discover their passions and take ownership of some responsibility in the group. We also keep Hosts watching for and delegating tasks to upcoming leaders, whom we refer to informally as *Future Hosts* (some may call them apprentices or coleaders). We identify people's roles of responsibility in a relational environment through their practical functions, not through titles.

We identify Hosts and their small groups in four categories, each requiring different amounts and types of care:

- *New groups.* These receive priority care. We know the devil likes to kill things young (like when he used Pharaoh in trying to kill baby Moses and Herod in trying to kill baby Jesus), so we give new groups proactive care, as they are the most vulnerable. These Hosts receive three contacts from Community Leaders (coaches) within their first six weeks, and then we evaluate next steps for the Host and the group. We encourage a new Host to complete CLASS 101.

- *Seasoned groups.* These receive personal care. Their Hosts have completed Leader Training 1 (described later), understand personal and group health, and have signed the Host Covenant. They are seasoned, but we still give them proactive monthly care.

- *Veteran groups.* These receive preferred care. Their Hosts have completed Leader Training 2, have established a group plan, and implement their plan for group health. They choose how we interact with them monthly—personally or by cell, email, text, or social media. They have earned the right to be trusted.

- *Stubborn groups.* These receive persistent care. These Hosts are late adopting our paradigm because they are either cautious or skeptical. We still love them and make monthly calls to pray with them, satisfied to leave prayers as messages if they don't answer.

Leader Coaches

Coaches are the experienced "leaders of leaders," and they become important as soon as a small group ministry grows beyond the point person's ability to care relationally for the small group leaders. At Saddleback we call our coaches Community Leaders (CLs), and they build relationships with a handful of Hosts, coming alongside to provide the care that I described above.

Some of our CLs specialize in one category of small group, and others care for a mix of categories. Aside from the CL's preferences, geography plays the largest role in assigning small groups to each CL. The ratio of CL to groups varies, depending on the category of groups. One CL can typically care for about twenty-five small groups of mixed categories.

Saddleback's small group ministry is large enough that we have another layer of leaders, called Small Group Pastors, who care for CLs. Though every connection should be relational, at this level our Small Group Pastor's dealings with CLs can be more "minister to minister," since CLs are experienced and fully committed and need a different relational process than Hosts.

Throughout this book I refer to all of the leaders between the small group point person (or pastor) and small group leaders as "infrastructure."

Small Group Point Person

This is probably you—the volunteer or paid staff who directly oversees the small group ministry. This person develops and implements the plan for the small group ministry as the house-to-house component of church life, keeping in view any or all of this book's five phases or "home" areas as they apply to their church paradigm (chapters 5–9). They build health in their groups and guard against drift, keeping the ministry's development on course, working *on* the ministry more than *in* it. For any size church I recommend the point person share the oversight task by developing a team of key ministry leaders who help work *on* the ministry. I call this the C Team.

The C Team

Most businesses have a C Suite—the CEO, CFO, COO, CTO, and so on—the top executives, the brain trust that keeps the business on track. Rather than "suite," I prefer the word "team" from the sports arena, where one person calls the plays and a team makes it happen. Each player knows his or her role, and together they are better than the individual. You will always be the one driving the process forward, but eventually you will need people around you.

When I first started at Saddleback, I performed all the functions that my C Team now performs. I later realized that by not giving away the ministry, I was hurting myself and robbing others of opportunities to use their giftedness and pursue their passions. Furthermore, we all need cheerleaders. We're more likely to do anything difficult—working out, dieting, keeping a commitment—when someone else does it with us. You'll find both motivation and wisdom in a team with which you connect in relationships. This team is so important that I will share about it in depth.

Your leader coaches may make good C Team members, but often not. Most coaches are high on caring and low on planning, and your C Team needs some strong planners. In your search for your C Team, don't overlook anyone anywhere in your small groups or in your church. For these roles, you should be more concerned about gifting than where people have fit historically in your organization.

Look for *capability* and *availability*. Capable C Team members are passionate about their responsibilities on the team and appropriately gifted. As for availability, I have discovered that passionate people don't always look at their calendars before committing. As much as it may pain you, make sure your recruits have time to do the job right or you'll end up with nothing more than a name on a line. Asking the hard questions up front will pay off in the long run.

Choose people who think holistically about your small group ministry. They need to help develop effective infrastructure to support small group leaders. Some of my C Team members also serve as Small Group Pastors or Community Leaders, but the C Team is so important that I don't expect its members to do double duty.

Just as relational connection is vital within your ministry, it is also vital between your ministry and other church ministries. Your C Team can help as ambassadors to senior church leadership and other ministries, helping cultivate buy-in from your entire church for your small group vision and mission. So it's important that every C Team member "gets" the big picture of your ministry, is able to relate well with other influencers, and positively impacts your church culture.

As the structure of this book reflects, I think of small group ministry planning in terms of five phases or "home" areas (chapters 5–9)— connecting, growing, investing, reaching, and sustaining. I recommend recruiting C Team members who specialize in different aspects of ministry planning and development, ideally matching each member's responsibilities with his or her passions, experience, and gifting. This is where you become a human resources expert, finding the best person to help you strategize and execute your plans in one aspect of your ministry strategy.

For example, ideal C Team members specializing in the connecting phase may be especially talented at creating cohesive groups. Though they are encouraging relationships within all groups, they themselves are likely to have energetic, "magnetic" personalities that draw the unconnected people. They love customer service and follow-up. They can easily adjust to various situations and can read the room effectively to help everyone feel welcome. Does this bring anyone to your mind? Jot down any likely names below. Commit to praying about them and whether to invite them to the team.

You may want to come back to this part of the book after you have read the questions each phase entails. As you read those chapters, come back and think of a name for your C Team member if one doesn't come to mind now.

I cannot overstate the importance of prayer in this. Pray for wisdom as the Lord brings people to your mind. Review each distinct area of ministry responsibility, and pray for the Lord's wisdom to bring the right person for that job. Don't be discouraged if you don't find everyone right away. Take your time, and let God reveal who he wants to bring alongside you.

Your ministry paradigm may differ somewhat from the paradigm in this book, but you will probably need faithful people to oversee most or all of these five areas. Prayerfully brainstorm names for:

Connecting (starting groups, placing new members)

_____

_____

_____

_____

Growing (fostering spiritual health in groups)

_____

_____

_____

_____

Investing (ensuring kingdom fruit from groups)

_____

_____

_____

_____

Reaching (encouraging group outreach)

_____

_____

Sustaining (maintaining long-term ministry success)

I also recommend another kind of variety in your C Team. Let me introduce this by quoting 1 Peter 5:1–4:

> To the *elders* among you, I appeal as a fellow elder and a witness of Christ's sufferings who also will share in the glory to be revealed: Be *shepherds* of God's flock that is under your care, watching over them [serving as *overseers*]—not because you must, but because you are willing, as God wants you to be; not pursuing dishonest gain, but eager to serve; not lording it over those entrusted to you, but being examples to the flock. And when the Chief Shepherd appears, you will receive the crown of glory that will never fade away. (emphasis added)

This passage uses three different words for church leaders: *elders*, *shepherds*, and *overseers*. These are used interchangeably to describe the same leaders, but they reflect different aspects of spiritual leadership, and individuals tend to be stronger in one than the others. Let's do a little Greek study to fully understand the nuanced differences between these.

"Elder" is translated from the Greek *presbuteros*, after which the Presbyterian denominations are named. They call their leaders "elders." In spite of its literal meaning, in the Bible "elder" does not necessarily mean physically old. It implies spiritual maturity. Timothy was a young man, yet he was pastor and elder at the church of Ephesus. Paul told him, "Don't let anyone look down on you because you are young" (1 Tim. 4:12), so anyone with spiritual maturity may qualify to be an elder. Elders lean toward being visionary. They are wise, and they develop wisdom and character in others.

The Greek word *poimēn* is translated "pastor" or "shepherd," and it refers to those who care for, lead, and feed the Lord's flock. Shepherds gravitate toward nurturing people in relationship. They pull people in and tend to exhibit magnetic personalities.

And "overseer" is translated from the Greek *episkopos*, which is translated "bishop" in the King James Version. The Episcopal denominations derive their name from *episkopos*, and they refer to their leaders as bishops, whose responsibility is to preside over local pastors or parish priests. Overseers are the process people. They are managers who put strategic plans into motion. This is my specialty. I love the planning process, developing programs, and being strategic. You will see this unfold throughout this book.

We all know that different churches use these words differently. That's not my concern here. I want to consider the three kinds of behavioral traits that all contribute to spiritual leadership. Each of us gravitates to one more than the others. The lines between the three are blurry, and that's okay because we don't all fit neatly into boring little boxes.

Now what about you? Toward which of these three roles do you gravitate? Think through the roles of elder, shepherd, and overseer, and take a few minutes to self-evaluate. Once you determine which role best describes you, do your best also to prayerfully evaluate which strengths best describe others you may recruit to your C Team, and write their names below. Make sure your team contains a mix of all three, but especially be sure to recruit team members who balance your tendencies.

Elder (vision)

_____

_____

_____

Shepherd (caring)

_____

_____

_____

_____

Overseer (management)

_____

_____

_____

_____

Support Elsewhere in Your Church

Besides your C Team, you want to continue to identify key influencers in your church who can be your ministry allies, and you theirs. Obviously your senior pastor should be one, and you should already be nurturing that relationship, but who else in your church needs to become passionate for what you're trying to do? These people hold a stake in the church's direction and success, and if your ministry is helping your church succeed, help them see that supporting your ministry is in their own best interest. (Also, take an active interest in supporting their ministry.)

Work those relationships, because you should not be championing small groups on your own. And as these relationships grow, you are fostering trust, which will allow you to speak and receive truth as needed. In fact, I advise you to start building key relationships well before you start present-ing your vision, mission, and requests for your ministry.

Support for You Beyond Your Church

Over my thirty-plus years in ministry I have gathered much knowledge and many great ideas from other churches of all sizes. (Never, ever stop learn-ing. You can learn from every size ministry and every style of leader.) It's a good idea to get to know churches in your area and meet with their pastors and ministry leaders. We started the international Small Group Network, and there we facilitate "Huddles" of leaders from different churches. Visit www.SmallGroupNetwork.com to find one in your area.

Rather than competing, we are all playing on the same team and striv-ing toward the same end goal: to bring people to Jesus Christ. Commit to working with other churches to strengthen leaders, broaden corporate influence, and create strong ministries that will ultimately build God's kingdom.

We also facilitate local or virtual Communities of Purpose (COPs) who gather monthly to hold each other accountable for executing their plans. These are peer-to-peer learning groups that meet virtually or physically, and you can go to www.SmallGroupNetwork.com/cop to find one in your area.

It is easy to become isolated and stand alone. Once you've distilled your specific plan and a few near-future goals from this book, if you are by yourself, you may put the plan on your shelf and soon drift off course. Connecting regularly with a COP will keep you focused and account-able to follow through. Your colleagues will also be there to help you stay upright through the rogue winds and storms of ministry when the devil wants to toss you around. Pastor Rick says, "I grew up in Northern California near the giant redwoods. Redwood trees have shallow roots. They withstand the wind by intertwining roots and holding each other up. What a perfect picture of fellowship!" We spread out, we intertwine, and we hold each other up. That's what the Small Group Network's COP can do for you.

Following is a great story from Brian Naess and Steve Curran, explaining how their Community of Purpose worked for them. First, from Brian, pastor of outreach and assimilation at Violet Baptist Church, Violet, Ohio:

> One of the most valuable parts of the Accelerate! conference is connecting with accountability groups [COPs]. We commit to meeting once a month for a year. These times have been invaluable for me to carry out what I learned. Even more than that, I have gained an incredible friend, Steve Curran, from Georgia of all places, to do ministry together. We have just completed our year commitment and have decided to continue meeting.

And from Steve, Life Groups team leader at Compassion Christian Church, Savannah, Georgia:

> I have been in a small group ministry for a number of years and had a ministry plan firmly in place. I came away from Accelerate! with new clarity of vision for small groups at my church. Every bit of that was worth the trip, but the added and unexpected bonuses are the new relationships. We were each paired with an accountability partner [in a COP], and we committed to praying for and remaining in contact with that person on a monthly basis. My partner, Brian Naess, is an incredible encourager, a great sounding board, and a godly man who has become a true friend. Although Brian and I have passed our one-year mark, we still talk every month. He has helped me stay the course and run my race well. The practical tools from Accelerate!, as well as my friendship with Brian, have really accelerated my ministry.

You can join a COP group now at www.SmallGroupNetwork.com/cop. It's free, and it's waiting for you!

Handle with Prayer

God has placed you here, at this time. Never have these words from Philippians 1:6 held more truth: "I am sure that God who began the good work within you will keep right on helping you grow in his grace until his task within you is finally finished on that day when Jesus Christ returns"

(TLB). Kevin Pent, church life pastor at Forward Church in Cambridge, Ontario, recently emailed me: "I'm starting a five-day fast today and would appreciate your prayers. Looking forward to what God's going to do through everyone who attended the Accelerate! conference. First things first though—prayer! God bless!" First thing—prayer! These are words to live by, and exactly the way you should approach every step of your ministry. Prayer will help you stay the course and maintain the correct perspective.

As you do a good thing, Satan will be working against you. Everything of value that we do is a spiritual battle. Most often a spiritual high is followed by a spiritual battle. The sooner you realize this, the more prepared you will be. In Ephesians 6:10–20, Paul describes the character qualities and spiritual practices that protect us in battle and pave the way to victory. He concludes with a strong emphasis on prayer, for oneself and for others:

> And pray in the Spirit on all occasions with all kinds of prayers and requests. With this in mind, be alert and always keep on praying for all the Lord's people. Pray also for me, that whenever I speak, words may be given me so that I will fearlessly make known the mystery of the gospel, for which I am an ambassador in chains. Pray that I may declare it fearlessly, as I should. (Eph. 6:18–20)

I could fill this book with examples of Satan working against my ministry, so I make sure I always have others praying for me. These people are not always the *who's who* of the church, but they love the Lord and know the value of intercession. They bring my needs relationally and conversationally to the Lord and are more concerned about bringing these needs to the Lord than fixing them. I look for people who are more excited about praying than fully knowing what they are praying for. Yes, I want them to pray specifically, but some people are mainly motivated to know "the inside scoop," and that's not the kind of people I need.

Take a moment and jot down the names of five people you will invite to pray for you and your ministry:

Now take the next step. Email, call, or text them right now and ask that they commit to pray for you weekly. Your job will be to update them regularly so they will know how to continue praying for you. Through this commitment you will draw closer to them, and you won't find yourself leading alone. Your prayer team will provide the spiritual covering you so desperately need.

3

Lead Effectively

Some aspects of leadership in a small group ministry are unique to that type of ministry, and we will touch on many of these later. But some leadership principles apply across all ministries, and we will deal with several of those broader concepts in this chapter. These affect not only you as the small group point person, but also all of those in various leadership roles. Part of your job is to build these into your whole leadership team and frequently revisit the most important points.

Keep It in the Family

Your church and your ministry should be run like a family, not a corporation, government, or school. God designed the church as a family system—so much so that the greatest qualification for a pastor is managing a family (1 Tim. 3:5). Throughout the New Testament, the motifs are parent/child, not teacher/pupil. And even families have to guard against overcontrol. High control naturally leads to rebellion, and the church is not immune to this. I can't overstate that you must let the Holy Spirit do his job, which frees you up from thinking you have to dictate everything. The Bible is written on a family system.

Remember that God is the architect of your ministry. You can be the general contractor, but you are following *his* blueprints. Any project typically encounters hitches and delays. Don't let them discourage you. God will provide the people and the tools to complete the job according to his purpose.

The Bible is written on a family system.

Although Saddleback is a large church, we are structured like a family. We have found this a much more effective and efficient way to function biblically. You may read and hear about some concepts that sound similar to those used in corporations, governments, or schools. However, we implement everything in our church, and in our small group ministry, as a family would, as described in the New Testament.

Become an Influencer

Are you a thermometer or a thermostat? A thermometer measures the temperature, but a thermostat *sets* the temperature. If you use your influence in the right way, you will be a thermostat, not a thermometer. The definition of *influencer* is someone who has the power to affect how someone else develops, behaves, or thinks. Each one of us has some level of influence through such simple means as conversations, emails, or texts, and especially through your actions. Your influence can be positive or negative.

Influence is not about a position or recognized authority. We've all seen someone whose authority is "increased," and yet it hasn't affected their influence at all. Neither is influence about wealth or fame. It is, however, all about how God uses you in relationships. Jesus said, "Let your good deeds shine out for all to see, so that everyone will praise your heavenly Father" (Matt. 5:16 NLT). God will use whatever you have if you let him.

Be cautious not to use your influence for personal benefit. Misuse of your influence will affect your credibility and the trust others place in you. Just as a lender discerns whether your credit is sufficient for your loan amount, people examine your life to determine whether you are worthy of their trust.

The fastest way to influence is likability. This may seem elementary, but trust is a by-product of a positive impression. If you like people and they like you, your sphere of influence will increase. Now you can like people while still disagreeing with them. We can "agree to disagree." So keep your relational attitude loving, especially when opinions differ. Then your influence will continue to be positive, enhancing the forward momentum of your ministry.

Cold Authority Versus Relational Influence

Believe it or not, you can actually learn something from a presidential campaign. Candidates are masterful at building relationships with their target audience—both those who are on board as well as the demographic they need to attract. Contrast this with a military campaign that is autocratic, not at all relational, and quite often leads to a coup. Which campaign style do you see as the most effective in your ministry? Relationship always wins.

You must grasp when and how to effectively exercise your authority in a relational context. When you're working with a team, God will use you, the point person, to make final decisions after accepting input from the team, and sometimes those decisions won't be popular. These are times when you must exercise your authority, but you can minimize resistance and resentment if your normal pattern is most often relational influence, not just dictating from a distance.

I keep coming back to the concept of a family. I can try to influence my kids to do their homework by talking over the reasons it is important, then leaving the decision up to them. And that's fine when they do the wise thing. But sometimes I simply have to exercise my positional authority and tell them to go do their homework.

Whether followers understand or not, the effective leader must sometimes make executive decisions. Don't be afraid to do this when it's right and necessary. Do what is right, not just what is easy. But your authoritative decisions will receive the greatest trust and acceptance when your followers know that you love them because you've often worked with them through loving influence in authentic relationships.

Do what is right, not just what is easy.

Two Guardrails

The success of your ministry depends on two important guardrails that keep your small groups on the pathway to producing mature disciples, according to your church's definition (see Q5 in chapter 6). For Saddleback, a mature disciple has a heart that balances Jesus's Great Commission and great commandment. Small groups tend to start out of balance. The guardrails help ensure that the group initiators move toward the balance our church wants for them, so they will produce mature disciples (see figure 3.1).

One guardrail is what I call *head* or *processes*. This has to do with the more factual and intellectual aspects—leader training, ministry tools, and video curriculum (discussed in Q6, Q7, and Q9). These processes help group members understand the group's functional purpose and how to succeed at it. The other guardrail I call *heart* or *people*. This is the relational component, including, for example, the loving coaching of our Community

Figure 3.1

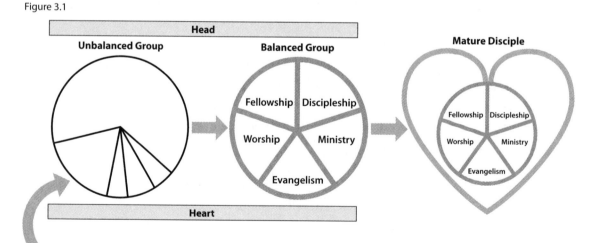

Leaders (Q7) who give sacrificially of their time to flesh out the intellectual training in the lives of our Hosts. This also brings the relational side to our use of data in tracking and caring for groups and their members (Q4).

Together, these guardrails will keep your small groups on course, producing the kinds of disciples your church is after.

I also try to adhere to this leadership policy: the shepherd, not the sheep, picks the next pasture. While you often need input from others, the final decisions are yours, and you shouldn't abdicate your calling to lead the small group ministry. It is your job to guide your flock, not let the flock guide you. Through the Old and New Testaments we see that it is the calling of the pastor to guide the sheep. The shepherd has insight from a unique perspective, different from that of the sheep, as to where God wants to take the flock. It is your job to lead through the planning process, from your current "pasture" to the pasture you see in your vision, along a specific path toward a chosen end. Of course there is wisdom in many counselors. You need wise people around you (your C Team, church leadership, etc.), and you must listen and learn. Just don't turn it into a democracy.

The shepherd, not the sheep, picks the next pasture.

Saddleback's Top Ten Small Group Ministry Commitments[1]

Over the years we have been asked for guidance about starting, leading, and sustaining a healthy small group ministry. Trust me when I tell you, we haven't always done it right, nor have we figured it all out. But one of the things I deeply love about our church, staff, and members is their willingness to keep evaluating throughout the journey, and even more, their readiness to course correct if needed. We *always* lead with prayer, seeking the will of God.

Together our ministry team came up with these commitments to keep us on target. These aren't just for me as the small group point person; I make sure they serve to guide all leaders throughout our ministry. Once you've chosen the commitments that will guide your ministry, make sure your whole small group ministry team knows and owns them.

1. I will move slowly.

One of the worst things you can do is read a book or attend a conference and try to immediately implement all that you've learned. Quick action often risks triggering land mines. Don't assume you know your ministry environment until you've listened carefully to its stakeholders. Change requires time, especially in a church environment.

> Only simpletons believe everything they're told!
> The prudent carefully consider their steps.
> The wise are cautious and avoid danger;
> fools plunge ahead with reckless confidence.
> (Prov. 14:15–16 NLT)

Before you take a step, *pray*! Then pause and listen for God's direction. This direction could come from multiple sources, including your quiet time, friends, people in your ministry, church leaders, and elsewhere. Seek to understand the people around you, and work with them. Commit to not moving over them in your enthusiasm, but rather moving together with them toward God's end purpose. Moving slowly doesn't mean you're intimidated or fearful, but that you are thoughtful and intentional.

2. I will regularly check my motives and evaluate my heart.

Does your ministry come from a pure motive, or are you climbing the ministry ladder and merely checking things off your to-do list? Are you serving God or feeding your ego? Do you feel compassion toward those you are serving, or are they simply interruptions in your day?

Jesus provided a good model:

I am the Good Shepherd. The Good Shepherd puts the sheep before himself, sacrifices himself if necessary. A hired man is not a real shepherd. The sheep mean nothing to him. He sees a wolf come and runs for it, leaving the sheep to be ravaged and scattered by the wolf. He's only in it for the money. The sheep don't matter to him. (John 10:11–13 MSG)

Luke 19:41 describes Jesus's example of compassion. He wept over Jerusalem and all the lost people. You must lead with this same compassion.

Your motivation must be God-centered, and you need to fully rely on him. We are all human and need affirmation and recognition. But "sooner or later we'll all have to face God, regardless of our conditions. We will appear before Christ and take what's coming to us as a result of our actions, either good or bad" (2 Cor. 5:10 MSG). Make sure you create and strengthen your ministry to glorify God and to enhance people's spiritual health and effectiveness.

3. I will steer clear of the numbers game.

If a man has a hundred sheep and one of them wanders away, what will he do? Won't he leave the ninety-nine others on the hills and go out to search for the one that is lost? (Matt. 18:12 NLT)

It does not matter how many groups you have or the size of your church. Never evaluate based solely on numbers but also on the health of each group and the ministry as a whole. God uses every church, regardless of size, to bring people to his Son, Jesus. Of course you must keep records to help you track progress and plan next steps, but avoid using numbers for bragging rights. Pay more attention to the measurable health of your groups. *Evaluate by health, not just numbers!* (We'll look more closely on measuring progress in chapter 5.)

4. I will not criticize the past.

Every teacher . . . is like the owner of a house who brings out of his storeroom new treasures as well as old. (Matt. 13:52)

Regardless of the current status of your small group ministry, it is an indication of the foundation that was likely built by someone else. Honor that foundation, regardless of your own personal opinions. Your role is to build on the foundation, not destroy it. Never criticize the past. Your character is revealed when you honor predecessors: "God used them for his purpose." Also, I believe that history provides a plethora of learning

65

opportunities. Examine the past, pick out the pearls, and learn from what didn't work out as planned.

5. I will avoid the comparison trap.

> Pay careful attention to your own work, for then you will get the satisfaction of a job well done, and you won't need to compare yourself to anyone else. (Gal. 6:4 NLT)

It is human nature to compare ourselves to others, and unfortunately the church is not immune to this. It is sinful to feel superior to another church or ministry, which is pride. Comparison can also make you feel discouraged, which can result in envy. Neither outcome is productive or helpful, and both will end up damaging your ministry. God created a unique fingerprint for each church and ministry, so learn from others but let your ministry be the healthy, unique version God intends. Always be ready to learn from larger, smaller, and otherwise different churches and ministries. Discover and act on God's special purpose for you, and don't waste time trying to slavishly re-create some other church or ministry.

6. I will focus on priorities and exercise a faith worth imitating.

When Jesus was asked what the most important commandment in the law of Moses was, he replied,

> "You must love the LORD your God with all your heart, all your soul, and all your mind." This is the first and greatest commandment. A second is equally important: "Love your neighbor as yourself." The entire law and all the demands of the prophets are based on these two commandments. (Matt. 22:37–40 NLT)

The Lord is clear about our priorities. Never lose sight of love for God and for people as you work to create and grow your ministry. Taking action on your priorities takes faith and dependence on God to do great things. Ask yourself if you have a faith worth imitating. If someone was handed your spiritual life for seventy-two hours, afterward would that person desire to hang on to your faith or prefer to give it back?

You should never do anything in ministry alone. You need people around you to strengthen your faith so you can focus on priorities. We help each other maintain perspective and can redirect each other if we lose our way. Sharing your responsibility with a team gives you more time to reflect and pray for God's direction so you don't lose your priorities in the noise around you, which can erode your faith.

7. I will pace myself.

Let us not become weary in doing good, for at the proper time we will reap a harvest if we do not give up. (Gal. 6:9)

It is possible to do ministry at such a pace that your work *for* God can destroy the work *of* God. We need to keep the long game in view, not just quick results. We can get so caught up in daily demands that we forget the habits that ensure endurance. Don't be person who says, "I didn't have time to pray today because I was late for a prayer meeting." Religious activity can easily replace spiritual intimacy.

If you are not spiritually, mentally, emotionally, and physically aligned with God and his purpose, your heart begins to harden and you start to burn out. It is difficult, especially while building a new ministry, to pace yourself and live for the long game. You may feel guilt or frustration if you aren't achieving "enough" progress. It's natural to see a rhythm of productive and nonproductive days, and you have to determine when to take a break because rest is part of God's rhythm for endurance. Stress is the fruit when your professional life dictates your personal self-care, rather than self-care supporting your professional success.

8. I will serve.

Whoever wants to become great among you must be your servant, and whoever wants to be first must be your slave—just as the Son of Man did

> *It is possible to do ministry at such a pace that your work for God can destroy the work of God.*

not come to be served, but to serve, and to give his life as a ransom for many. (Matt. 20:26–28)

The most important part of leadership is a servant's heart. This is countercultural, but Jesus was countercultural. And isn't our goal to be Christlike? No job is too big or too small when setting up and maintaining your ministry. Lead by example and serve those around you, "just as the Son of Man did not come to be served, but to serve."

9. I will be a learner.

> Walk with the wise and become wise;
>> Associate with fools and get in trouble. (Prov. 13:20 NLT)

I am a firm believer in the acquisition of knowledge. Your first resource must be the Word of God, chock-full of wisdom crucial to building a God-honoring ministry. I also believe you can learn from everyone—either what to do or what *not* to do. Seek counsel from those who have gone before you; ask questions of those around you; read books or attend conferences that relate to your ministry. Never become so certain of your way that you miss clear direction from God. All good leaders are learners. (Chapter 6 will offer many available learning opportunities.)

10. I will stay focused and never give up.

> Let us strip off every weight that slows us down, especially the sin that so easily trips us up. And let us run with endurance the race God has set before us. (Heb. 12:1 NLT)

You are never a failure until you give up, and it's always too soon to quit. Regardless of your position in the church, commit to helping people connect in relationships and grow spiritually healthy. I've endured many days and seasons of frustration when nothing seemed in harmony. I couldn't afford to dwell on the frustrating moments, or I would have become a frustrated person. I had to learn that trials teach lessons, and then I could focus on contentment even in the midst of trouble. I love Psalm 62:5–6: "My soul, wait in silence for God only, for my hope is from Him. He only is my rock and my salvation, my stronghold; I shall not be shaken" (NASB). Focus on what you know is truth: God is in control! (Chapter 9 is all about sustaining long-term success.)

Always Forward, with Patience

Some of the commitments above, taken the wrong way, may lead some to hesitate or stall out. But someone once said, "If you're satisfied, you're standing still. And if you're standing still, you're going backward." Yes, sometimes we need times of stillness and silence to shut out life's distracting noise and find fresh direction. But then we must emerge from these retreats in order to keep progressing and changing toward the Lord's purpose.

It is easy and very common for churches to get stuck in "we've always done it this way." Or "if it ain't broke, don't fix it." But I say *break it* if it doesn't keep you going forward. The world is moving faster and faster, so churches must remain dynamic and evolving, while clinging to the truths of God's Word. If we become satisfied or self-righteous in our habits, we run the risk of stagnancy. Then the world and the opportunity to reach the world—the higher stakes—will pass without a backward glance.

This may overwhelm you. You may feel you're racing the clock to set up your ministry. But God's timing may be different from yours. Your progress may seem to take forever, but I assure you, if you are serving faithfully, God is working even when you feel stalled. If you are task-oriented (as I am), this waiting time can be torturous, but there's always something you can continue to do even as you wait on the Lord. Do it steadfastly, patiently, expectantly.

Make Meetings Count

Whether we like it or not, "doing church" means meetings. Sure, many of us have too many meetings, but too few meetings can create a lack of communication. People are down on what they are not up on. So with any group, make sure your meetings have purpose and fulfill that purpose.

Any leadership team meeting is critical, yet team leaders seldom plan for efficient, effective meetings. With any of my ministry leaders, I like to call them a "team" rather than "staff" to emphasize the need to work cohesively together. My teams understand that every individual is an important part of the whole.

Meetings can easily get off purpose because we all like to talk. Therefore, all purposeful meetings require knowing *where* you are taking the team, *what* you want to accomplish, and *why* you gather.

Know *where* you *are taking* your *team.*

Look ahead six to twelve months and determine what skills or character traits your team needs to strengthen in order to travel those months in a healthy, effective way. How does your team need to improve? Only you as the leader can lead, so where do you want to take the team over the next year? I usually start praying, inviting input from people, and planning for each year in October, well before I roll everything out in January. I set up a theme for each year that largely defines the overarching shape and direction of weekly team meetings. For some examples of previous themes, see www.SmallGroups.net/theme.

Know *what* you *want to accomplish.*

For leadership meetings at all levels, I use a framework that includes three components: *devotional* (spiritual, heart, vision), *celebrational* (team, individuals, rhythms), and *practical* (housekeeping, news, reminders, upcoming events). A different structure may better serve your team needs, but allow me to expand on my pattern.

We always start with God's Word. Our devotion time keeps our hearts in line and sets the tone for our meetings. I also request that team members take an active role in planning and leading our meetings. For instance, each member takes a week and creates a devotional based on his or her perspective of our annual theme. Devotionals can also include teachings related to our vision, or anything the Lord lays on our hearts. Our devotions are flexible in order to let the Lord lead.

After our devotional time we move into celebration and acknowledgment. We recognize personal and group accomplishments—maybe a successful conference or a goal reached. We celebrate birthdays and work anniversaries to affirm each member's importance. And we set a rhythm around regular annual events or seasons. Our January kickoff meeting includes a white elephant exchange at my house, where I unveil the year's theme. In July I reteach the year's theme, as we usually have new people on board, and this is a fun way to refresh our memories. In the summer we do Team Day to relax and bond. December closes out our year with a team Christmas party.

Finally, the practical meeting component includes housekeeping details and news about the church, our ministry, or other ministries. We also go through a list of reminders and upcoming events to keep us on track. We all have many irons in the fire, so review is important.

Know why you are gathering.

Your reason for gathering will help you answer many other questions. Is the meeting's purpose worth what it costs in time and dollars (perhaps for salaries or other costs)? Does everything in the meeting keep the team focused on the main thing—due north? Does everything add value to what you are trying to accomplish? Nobody wants just another meeting, but a meeting with purpose is a game changer!

Any meeting agenda can vary between highly structured to very loose, depending on the personality of the leader. Neither is wrong. The choice depends on the leader's God-given wiring. But regardless of your personality type, you need to stay flexible. If you gravitate toward structure, be open for the agenda to change. If you gravitate toward a looser style, don't "cop out" on prepping for the meeting or blame God if the meeting doesn't go well.

Don't get hung up on doing things a certain way every time. Read the mood of the team and adapt as needed. Are you coming off a major church push, or are you in the dog days of summer? Is a team member on a high or going through a low? Practice the art of adjusting to the need of the moment.

A few other things to keep in mind:

1. A meeting doesn't have to go the exact allotted time. It may go shorter; it may go longer. Plan extra uncommitted time after meetings so you can go longer if God is up to something that requires it. Extended meetings should be rare so your people don't feel you're in the habit of abusing their time.

2. It's okay to cancel a meeting. Sometimes your schedule, the church schedule, or other events make this wise or necessary.

3. As much as possible, establish a rhythm for team meetings—same week of the month, same day of the week, same time, same place, and so on. While irregularities are often wise and needed, consistency simplifies communication and strengthens team unity.

4

Lead with a Vision and Mission

Vision is your dream. Where do you want your ministry to go? What is your big picture of the future?

Mission is the purpose of your small group ministry. What, specifically, will you do to work toward fulfilling your dream?

What Is the Vision for Your Small Group Ministry?

As you start a new ministry or accelerate an existing ministry, you likely have a long list of things you *need* or tasks that *need* to be accomplished. I've found that need only goes so far in motivating people. They are often much more eager to help realize a God-inspired *vision* for a growing ministry or church. But churches often resort only to need in their appeals. I attended a conference at which we were given a flyer that listed all the needs for that ministry. Afterward the conference coordinators revealed that out of about 150 people, only one responded to the list of needs.

The conference attendees were called to a need, not a vision. Some people are wired to respond to needs, but don't depend exclusively on that motivation. If you also call your people to a vision—to the specific reasons they are there and the end you are seeking to accomplish for God's kingdom—they are more apt to respond and get involved.

Every successful leader has a vision in mind—something he or she is moving toward. People respond to that because vision is vital, not only to the leader, but also to the volunteer. A desperate need-based request typically doesn't recruit many people, but a well-thought-out vision will draw in more people and inspire them in ways you never thought possible.

Spiritual health will get you numbers, but numbers will not get you spiritual health.

Remember, it's crucial not to get hung up on numbers as you figure out your vision. Spiritual health will get you numbers, but numbers will not get you spiritual health. Your vision should emphasize dream. Our small group vision is to see every person, from the core of our church to the ever-growing community, connected to a healthy small group. Notice that the dream won't be realized by people's connection to just any small group, but to a *healthy* small group. We define a healthy group as one in which the members fellowship together, learn together, serve together, reach out together, and worship together. Combined, all those purposes create a healthy subculture of our church's larger community.

The vision for your ministry should reflect and serve the larger vision for your church. As examples, I'm including below the vision statements for our church and small group ministry. These may give you a starting point as you define the vision for your own ministry. Why, exactly, are we here?

Saddleback Church Vision

A great commitment to the great commandment and the Great Commission will grow a great church.

Saddleback Small Group Ministry Vision

To see every person, from the core of our church to the ever-growing community, connected in a healthy small group.

What Is the Mission of Your Small Group Ministry?

Once you have defined your vision, you must understand the mission of your small group ministry. If your vision is your *dream*, your mission is what you are going to *do*. What is the purpose of your small group ministry?

Most likely your church has a mission statement, or at least an unstated mission in the mind of your senior leadership. Make sure your small group ministry's mission aligns with that of your church and the direction of your senior pastor. Here are the mission statements of Saddleback Church and Saddleback's small group ministry:

Saddleback Church Mission
   To bring people to Jesus and membership in his family, develop them to Christlike maturity, and equip them for their ministry in the church and their life mission in the world in order to magnify God's name.

Saddleback Small Group Ministry Mission
   To balance the Great Commission and the great commandment in the hearts of every member and group.

We've carefully mapped out a spiritual growth pathway for all church attendees to travel, supporting each other in community toward the church's and ministry's mission. Our vision and mission provide our compass to keep us always pointed due north, in the right direction.

Stating Your Vision and Mission

The rest of this book will help you plan a small group ministry that will fulfill your vision and mission. But you need to start with a strong foundation. Without the vision and mission to guide you, the plan you develop through this book will not follow a clear direction.

Take a few minutes to evaluate your vision and mission for your small group ministry. Your first step is to look at your church's vision and mission in order that your ministry will line up with and support them. If you don't know your church's vision and mission, talk with your senior leaders and ask where they want the church to go and how your small group ministry can help the church go there. You don't want a situation where your ministry works in opposition to your church.

My dad always told me that in business you want to think of the whole company, not just your department. He was a Navy aviator, and though he flew planes off aircraft carriers, he was just as concerned with the maintenance of the carrier as that of his plane. A hole in the carrier would sink the whole thing, including his plane.

Line up your ministry to support your church, and the church will support your ministry. They work together.

It's hard to predict how long it will take to formulate your ministry vision and mission statements. Be deliberate and allow yourself the time to pray through every aspect of your ministry.

What if your church doesn't have a clearly defined vision or mission? Well, even if there's no formal written statement—maybe the culture doesn't care—I can guarantee the church has a dream and a purpose on which you can build! Interview your senior leaders about these, and start your planning based on what they share.

Write your church and ministry vision and mission statements below, or at least preliminary drafts. This will help clarify your next steps. Pray, dream, align to your church, and pull others into this process—especially your church's senior leadership and your ministry's key planners.

My Church Vision Statement

My Small Group Ministry Vision Statement (our dream—why we are here)

_____

_____

_____

_____

My Church Mission Statement

_____

_____

_____

_____

My Small Group Ministry Mission Statement (our purpose—what we do)

_____

_____

_____

_____

Phases of Planning

Once you've determined at least a provisional vision and mission for your ministry that is aligned with your senior leadership and guided by your church's vision and mission, your ministry's foundation is set. Take a deep breath, then launch full speed into planning your small group ministry. As I described in the introduction, I propose five phases or "home" areas in the planning process. These overlap because every part of the ministry influences all the rest, and planning is not always a linear process. You will probably go back and forth a few times and find yourself in the midst of a couple of areas at one time.

Use chapters 5–9 to help you design each aspect of your small group ministry:

1. The kitchen, where people *connect*
2. The family room, where people *grow*
3. The study, where people *invest*
4. The front door, where people *reach* others
5. The dining room, where family *sustains*

You may find yourself turning some unexpected corners, slowing down, speeding up, or sometimes having to stop right in the middle of planning to evaluate what is happening. This is all normal, so don't be discouraged. Let's jump right in.

PART 2

The Home

5

The Kitchen

CONNECTING PEOPLE THROUGH SMALL GROUPS

Q1—How Will You Align Your Ministry with Other Church Leadership and Ministries?

Q2—How Will You Communicate the Value of Groups to Your Church?

Q3—What Is Your Plan for Connecting People into Groups?

Q4—How Will You Measure Your Progress?

People often ask me what is a healthy measure of church attendees connected into groups. That's tough to answer because it depends partly on where you are and where you want to go. It also depends on how many people from the broader community, outside your church, you want to bring into groups.

If your church uses the model of both temple courts and house to house, both parts should work together to help as many people as possible from your community come to know Jesus. In this case, I advise small group point people to strive for an increase of people in healthy groups each year. Not every year will see a gain, but you should always strive for an annual gain.

When I first started at Saddleback, our long-term dream goal was to have a greater number of people connected in healthy small groups than attending the weekend services (which means bringing into small groups many people who do not attend church yet). At the time we had 30 percent, so we set a short-term goal for that year to reach 40 percent. We finally reached 110 percent in 2004, and now we are aiming toward a bigger goal—ten thousand healthy groups.

If you haven't recruited a C Team member who will be responsible for overseeing this aspect of your small group ministry, I suggest you do so prayerfully (see chapter 2, "Lead as a Team"). At this moment, your own name may be at the top of your recruitment list, but I encourage you to pray, "Lord, show me who has the gift of connecting people in a way that will glorify you and move this ministry forward with unity."

How Will You Align Your Ministry with Other Church Leadership and Ministries?

I encourage you to consider three aspects of alignment in planning your small group ministry. First, you should align your ministry with your church's senior leadership. Second, your ministry and the various other church ministries need to be aligned and understand each other's roles in the church. And third, you and your ministry team need to align your plans and activities with your small group vision and mission. This is why chapters 1 and 4 are so important.

Is Your Senior Leadership on Board?

One of the most discussed issues at our Small Group Network conferences is how to set up a small group ministry when the senior pastor or other key leaders are not on board. You need to set up your small groups in a way that aligns 100 percent with the vision of your church, and I want to show you seven tactics you can use to successfully work through any differences in vision that you may encounter. It's imperative to work as a team with all of your church leadership.

You must build out your small group ministry plan around your senior church leadership. Your senior pastor is most likely the church's visionary, so your job is to build your ministry plan in a way that implements his or her vision. This ensures action, not just hallucination. Keep focusing on action, because everything eventually distills down to *work*!

Take a moment and look back at the church leaders you listed near the end of chapter 1—those with whom you are prayerfully seeking unified cooperation. You may think of other names to add—key opinion leaders with whom you wish to build relational equity. The following qualities, attitudes, and practices will guide you in working with these leaders toward the goals of your small group ministry and your church. These must especially characterize you, the small group point person, but also others in your ministry leadership who will serve as your ministry's "ambassadors" to the rest of the church. Work hard to disseminate these throughout your ministry leadership structure.

Display Humility, Not Entitlement

When I'm training a church staff, I always say, "Seek to let others discover you, not to make yourself discovered." That means humility. View your service responsibility as an honor. Never assume you are entitled to your position.

You must earn the right to be heard by building relationships on mutual trust, not by insisting on your own way. Show yourself to be a friend, not a divisive competitor, with your fellow leaders. If you serve humbly and wait to be discovered, God will do incredible things.

Appeal to the Interests of Others

Appeal to the goals and interests of your senior leaders. The prophet Daniel encountered some precarious situations, as in Daniel chapter 1, where he was told to compromise his values and his relationship with God. But he appealed to the goals and interests of his leaders without compromising his own value system and objectives. He made a simple request for a ten-day test and left the final decision to the king's representative. It's an art to think through ways to present your request in a synergistic way, showing how your goals and interests align with those of others.

Also seek to understand your senior leadership's love languages, which vary within teams as they do in families. "The wise are known for their understanding, and pleasant words are persuasive" (Prov. 16:21 NLT).

Earn a Reputation for Responsibility and Respect

Proverbs 22:1 says, "Choose a good reputation over great riches; being held in high esteem is better than silver or gold" (NLT). You want to be the go-to person who, no matter what, is willing to stand in the gap and make sure things get done. Come prepared with solutions instead of just presenting problems as a complainer.

Prove yourself a team player, respecting and supporting others' values and goals as well as your own. Discover your senior leadership's goals, and accomplish those first.

It's easy to get fired up about a new program, like small groups, and hammer your ideas. But it's more effective to launch new programs and ideas by shaping your ministry to support the church's culture. And if the church culture needs to be changed, introduce your suggestions gradually and respectfully. Help win over senior leadership by showing how your ideas work in conjunction with theirs to accomplish everyone's goals. At Saddleback Church, though I was hired as the Small Group Pastor, I understood the importance of other activities—for example, baptisms and CLASSes—and I even worked to integrate these values into our small group ministry plan.

Be Honest

Leaders are capable of resorting to a dark side, doing anything to accomplish our agenda. But "we have renounced secret and shameful ways; we do not use deception, nor do we distort the word of God. On the contrary, by setting forth the truth plainly we commend ourselves to everyone's conscience in the sight of God" (2 Cor. 4:2).

A "white lie" is still a lie. We often "bend the truth," exaggerate, or make the situation appear more favorable than it really is. If you become known as vulnerably honest about your failures as well as your successes, your frailties as well as your strengths, you'll maintain secure relationships through good times and tough times.

Consider Your Timing

I can become extremely task-oriented and forget that not everyone is on my accomplishment speedway at that moment. The minute I see Rick, I want to talk with him about my latest thoughts. I've learned to gauge where he is mentally before I bombard him with my agenda. For example, trying to talk to him before a service is pointless because, shockingly, he's focused on the service, not on me.

You'd be surprised how many people choose the workday equivalent to a toddler's bedtime for deep conversations. We get fired up and rush into lengthy, complicated conversations at the worst times.

Trust God

If your senior leadership rejects your ideas, trust God! Proverbs 3:5–6 says, "Trust in the LORD with all your heart and lean not on your own understanding; in all your ways submit to him, and he will make your paths straight." Trust that God has you in the right place and that he always accomplishes his will. If you're pressing the accelerator and your leaders seem to be stomping on the brake, it's okay—God has the wheel.

Remember Your True Identity

Your identity must be firmly rooted in Jesus Christ. Regardless of your ministry, you have to know that your identity, your calling, is in Jesus. You never know when ministry breakthrough is going to happen, but your faithfulness under all circumstances is the most important breakthrough, and you can ensure that now. Be patient in your other objectives; they sometimes take time. Don't give up.[1]

I hope these points will help you gain trust and alignment within your church. Seek God. Trust God. Obey God. He will move in others' hearts, and *his* will *will* be done!

Instructions for Question Planning Pages

After each of this book's twenty planning questions, you will find a question planning page to complete as part of your small group ministry plan. (You'll find the Q1 Planning Page immediately following these instructions.) I recommend completing these pages together with others from your church. We are better together!

Each question planning page offers ideas for three tasks you may do—a "crawl" task, a "walk" task, and a "run" task. These are presented at progressive difficulty levels to help you think developmentally. If the planning question presents a brand-new challenge, you may start with an easy crawl-level task. If your church has already wrestled through the question, consider an aggressive run-level task.

Each question planning page also provides a fillable chart with four planning steps: your dream, obstacles, actions, and timing.

Your Dream

Everything starts with a dream. When you first start, don't let problem solving creep in. Nothing destroys a dream quicker than limited human thinking. Give God a chance to show what he will do. Let your mind run wild with God-size faith. Word your dream as specifically as possible. For example, "I dream of 50 percent of our average attendance connected into small groups." If the dream doesn't scare you, it may not be big enough.

Feel free to dream long-term, beyond your next year, and write that dream under "Long-Term (1–5 years)." But it's hard to stay on track toward a long-term goal without breaking it down into intermediate steps. Refine your big dream into a series of smaller stages, and write these under "Short-Term (1–12 months)."

Obstacles

What might prevent you from reaching this dream? List anything and everything. For example, "Lack of good data about who is now in small groups."

Actions

Some of your action goals should be answers to obstacles. But think beyond fixing problems to proactive action goals. Example: "By the end of this month, research software for tracking group membership." In a moment I will explain the guidelines for effective SMART goals.

Nothing destroys a dream quicker than limited human thinking.

Timing

Think through your ideal completion date for each action goal. Will this take a week? A month? A quarter? A year? Make your best estimate and write in a date.

SMART Goals

At Saddleback we use **SMART** goals. This acronym first appeared in a November 1981 article in *Management Review* by George Doran, Arthur Miller, and James Cunningham.

S Is it *specific*? Does it define who, what, when, why, and how?

M Is it *measurable*? Is it quantifiable?

A Is it *action-oriented*? Does it describe actions to take?

R Is it *realistic*? Can you obtain the resources and cooperation to do it?

T Is it *timely*? Does it include a time frame for accomplishment?

Allow me to expand on these.

Specific

Don't word goals so vaguely that they offer no practical direction. A vague goal: "Grow small groups soon." A specific goal: "Add ten small groups by end of quarter."

Measurable

If you can't measure your progress, you may become discouraged, feeling you're getting nothing done. "Ten new groups" is measurable. "More groups" is not.

Action-Oriented

Write your goals in terms of actions to do, not just ends to reach. Example: "Implement fall promotion to add ten new groups by end of quarter."

Realistic

Always dream big! Stretch yourself, but understand the difference between an attainable goal of faith and something beyond all reason.

Timely

Include a time component so you don't wait indefinitely. This also provides accountability to move forward in a consistent manner.

The number of planning questions and the mountain of work they involve may overwhelm you. Don't be discouraged. I have guided hundreds of churches through this process. Don't be too concerned at first with the bigger picture of the whole plan. Work each question, one at a time. In chapter 10 I will guide you in pulling everything together into a *doable* twelve- to eighteen-month strategic plan. I promise!

Q1 Planning Page

Align with Other Leaders and Ministries

Please see pages 86–89, "Instructions for Question Planning Pages," for how to fill this out.

Suggested Tasks	**CRAWL**	**With other ministries:** *Meet with leaders of at least three other church ministries (outside your small group ministry) to build relationships and hear their stories and dreams.*
	WALK	**With key stakeholders:** *Meet with key church leaders and stakeholders to hear their stories, their take on the church's vision and mission, and their perception of the small group ministry.*
	RUN	**With your senior pastor:** *Schedule social and work-related meetings to build a relationship with your senior pastor. Seek to build trust and understand his or her vision before selling your ministry passion.*

Your Dream	Obstacles	Actions	Timing
Long-Range (1–5 years)			
Short-Range (1–12 months)			
	Other Actions		

After you've completed this page, mark the highest-priority action for this planning question. Copy that action onto the prioritizing list, pages 221–23 in chapter 10.

How Will You Communicate the Value of Groups to Your Church?

We are blessed at Saddleback Church because our senior leaders, especially Rick Warren, see the intrinsic value of our small group ministry. So although it isn't necessary to communicate the value of small groups to our leaders, it is still important to stress this to our church members. Rick frequently says, "If you want to be healthy and balanced, you need large group worship in the temple courts and small group fellowship in the home."

A recent article by Cade Metz related the pros and cons that Mark Zuckerberg sees in the Facebook community. According to Metz, Zuckerberg "says his model for an online community might look something like Saddleback. . . . The key for Zuckerberg is that Warren built a community in which tens of thousands of people gather under a capable leader's guidance, but also divide themselves into smaller groups by interest, affinity, and aspirations."[2] Facebook is this generation's biggest "crowd gather." But even Zuckerberg knows a crowd isn't a community, so he is planning the next step of community for Facebook. The church faces the same challenge, and we believe God has wisely addressed it in the house-to-house component of church, not just the temple courts.

Small group life offers many benefits on many levels, and your job is to communicate those benefits. Your small groups can be the heartbeat of your church, a source of your church's health and growth, a center for discipleship, a launch pad for evangelism, and a setting for worship and relationships.

When people spend time together in groups, they discover things about each other. Even casual conversations build trust and lead to exciting personal discoveries about people's gifts and other little facts that contribute to depth of relationships. Group members will also make sad or challenging discoveries about each other, but these are opportunities for support, encouragement, and healing. In groups people celebrate victories and carry each other through hard times. These require time together to develop intimacy as a safe environment for vulnerability.

Our fallen nature causes us to gravitate away from God, not toward him. Community is important because we help each other become better, putting what we learn into practice. The devil wants the opposite. Fear and isolation are the devil's playground. If he can isolate you or keep your relationships at a surface level, he wins. And he uses fear to make spiritual growth even harder than it already is. He keeps playing old tapes in your head: "You can't do it." "What will others think?" "You're a burden to your friends."

But in a healthy small group, we confront these lies with truth. Some of the ways you can communicate this and other benefits of small groups to your church include touch points, testimonies, timely sermons, and teaching pastors.

Touch Points

These are the places people interface with your church. Use them to help people understand the importance of small groups and relational community. They can include, but are not limited to:

1. Your church or ministry website, apps, and social media
2. Signage
3. Booths, kiosks, or ministry representatives in the church foyer or patio
4. Bulletins or response cards (paper or electronic) offering small group options

These are limited only by your creativity. Brainstorm ideas with your ministry team.

Testimonies

You are going to read over and over in this book the value of testimonies from "satisfied customers"—people who have benefited from small groups. You can put written or video testimonies on your website and use them in weekend services or other events. You can guide people to these by placing QR codes in your lobby and on printed literature.

Here's a great example from one of our thousands of small groups:

> My group of five years began with a core of nine members, and we've had some turnover. The fellowship is difficult to experience in any other setting. We are there for each other, we laugh together, and we get through difficult times together. We meet every Saturday for an in-depth study of James with interesting and thought-provoking discussions.
>
> Recently we welcomed a man from Iran. He was baptized several years ago, and when he went back to Iran, he was arrested and served several years in prison because of his faith. He lost his wife, and her parents kept his daughter from him. He felt safe with us when we accepted him unconditionally into our group family, where we maintain everything in confidentiality. We supported one couple during an extremely difficult time in their marriage, and they are now doing well. We're also supporting another member after her son's suicide.
>
> We started a closed Facebook page to share with each other any time, day or night. We serve together as often as possible and are praying about our small group family joining the Prison Ministry at Saddleback to reach out to those in dire circumstances and bring Jesus into their lives. As in any family, flexibility and open-mindedness have brought us this far.
>
> Finding the right small group has been a blessing beyond compare, essential to my spiritual growth. God works through us in so many ways, and we are without doubt so much better together.

Find testimonies from group leaders or members who clearly communicate the value of being part of a group that will ultimately become family. These come from your satisfied customers, and you, the salesperson, use them as a "selling tool." Whose word will best persuade new customers to buy?

Timely Sermons

Timely sermon series are also effective in communicating the value of small groups. Preaching on small groups and related topics is a great way to train your congregation in the value of community. The early chapters of Acts, on the birth of the church with its temple courts and house-to-house environments, can broaden the meaning of the word *church*. Or sermons on discipleship in our daily lives. Or a series on relational connection or the New Testament's fifty-eight uses of "one another." You can offer these in series or one-off sermons, perhaps coordinated with seasonal opportunities: New Year groups in January, Mom or Dad groups at Mother's Day and Father's Day, and so on. Think like Hallmark! They come up with all kinds of reasons to send cards.

Teaching Pastors

Utilize your teaching pastors and their personal experience in small groups. Rick often speaks about how his small group, through their "ministry of presence," held Kay and him together after their son Matthew died. A personal story is much more impactful than a sermon that just teaches ideas.

Q2 Planning Page

Communicate the Value of Groups

Please see pages 86–89, "Instructions for Question Planning Pages," for how to fill this out.

Suggested Tasks	**CRAWL**	**Touch points:** *Evaluate and plan your communications about groups, such as plugs during services, bulletin presence, web presence, a small group table manned by friendly representatives.*
	WALK	**Testimonies:** *Plan testimonies during services or on your website from people whose lives have been changed through small groups.*
	RUN	**Timely sermons:** *If and when you have the cooperation of senior and teaching pastors, coordinate a sermon series about values related to small groups as a way of getting people to join up.*

Your Dream	Obstacles	Actions	Timing
Long-Range (1–5 years)			
Short-Range (1–12 months)			
	Other Actions		

After you've completed this page, mark the highest-priority action for this planning question. Copy that action onto the prioritizing list, pages 221–23 in chapter 10.

What Is Your Plan for Connecting People into Groups?

You can't have a small group ministry without taking the initiative to motivate and recruit people to start or join groups. Understand this: *You must actively recruit for your small group ministry*. In order to motivate people to start or join small groups, you need to appeal to their felt need for relationship—that is, for relational connection, for fellowship, for belonging. The New Testament uses the metaphor of the human body: "Each of us has one body with many members, and these members do not all have the same function" (Rom. 12:4); and "From him the whole body, joined and held together by every supporting ligament, grows and builds itself up in love" (Eph. 4:16).

This story from Al and Bre, small group leaders from Saddleback's Anaheim campus, shows the value of connecting the right people with the right group:

> Bre and I prayed that the Lord would guide us to a small group that had families with young children, as well as people in the same stage of life. We felt God was leading us to start a group. We trusted that God would bring families with similar longings. That following weekend we took a leap of faith and signed up to host our own group. While we were signing up, we were told that two families had recently inquired about a small group specifically for families with small children. In our group we have seven children, ages one to twelve. Sure it's loud. Sure it's crazy. And sure the kids make a mess. But that is our group. God not only brought together a small group, he brought together a family!

You must actively recruit for your small group ministry.

Customer Service

As you connect people into groups, you will find yourself in the customer service business. You won't have enough time, staff, or energy to devote deep personal time to each person, but you still need to treat everyone with respect, making sure they know you value them. God is entrusting his children to your care, so care for them well. Steward God's people as valued individuals. Remember that people are not interruptions, but opportunities to build the oneness and maturity of Christ's body.

Why Multiplication Is Difficult for Connecting

We live in a fractured society. It is common for families to be scattered across the country due to demands of their jobs. I have four older brothers and an older sister; each one of us lives in a different state. Getting together as a family takes a lot of planning and traveling for everyone. As a result, it doesn't happen as frequently as we would like. If you have three children and send them off to college, the chances are very slim that all three will be able to come back to their hometown and find employment. Even if you live in a major city, the competition in the job market often forces people to move several states away for their career. The U.S. Census Bureau reports that the average American moves 11.7 times in his or her lifetime.[3]

In addition, divorce has become commonplace. The most frequently cited statistics state that somewhere between 40 and 50 percent of all marriages will end in divorce. Children are often forced to split their time between two households, sometimes traveling to different cities or even different states for visitation. Added to that, "fewer than half (46%) of U.S. kids younger than 18 years of age are living in a home with two married heterosexual parents in their first marriage."[4] As a result, many of us are growing up without a strong, positive role model of family or true community.

When you gather a group of Christians together and encourage them to meet weekly for a year and form strong bonds, it should be no surprise to learn that once they find community in a small group, they are reluctant to invite newcomers into the group and risk losing that sense of community. The small group has become the family they never had. In addition, birds of a feather flock together. Many Christians will tell you they don't even know any non-Christians beyond the grocery store clerk or gas station attendant, and it is a bit difficult to strike up a meaningful

Remember that people are not interruptions, but opportunities to build the oneness and maturity of Christ's body.

conversation while buying groceries or paying for gas. While it may be an exaggeration to say that most Christians don't know any non-Christians, research has found that once a person becomes a Christian, his or her circle of non-Christian friends decreases dramatically.

We are starved for community and seek experiences and situations that make us feel grounded and part of something. It is not too much of a stretch to imagine that a small group can provide this type of community. Fellowship, and the relationships it develops, fills a need. I know many people who say they are closer to their small group members than they are to their blood relatives.

As the small group becomes the modern form of biblical family, this creates the tension to introduce a rigid multiplication system.

When Addition Is Better Than Multiplication

Small group ministries live in constant tension between the safety of familiarity and the need to draw unconnected people into groups. We want small group members to develop deep relationships with each other, but we also need to integrate new people into groups. Many churches handle integration of new people by adding new members to an existing group until it reaches a certain size, then "multiplying" (splitting) it into two small groups, which can then grow and split again. But the unfortunate result is often members' resentment at the intrusions and forced splits. And the small group point person becomes frustrated continually trying to sell a concept that group leaders and members simply don't buy. We have found that it is better for all concerned to start new groups than for existing groups to multiply.

So how do we integrate new people? Largely through annual campaigns (described below). We have grown to more than seven thousand small groups by using campaigns to launch new groups each year. Since 2002 campaigns have increased small group participation from 30 percent to 110 percent! Since 2004 we have had more people in small groups than attend our weekend services. Rather than taking energy away from our small groups by forced "multiplication" (division), the campaign approach focuses on relationships. Now we are praying for ten thousand healthy small groups!

Outside our annual campaigns, when people express interest in a small group, we offer two courses of action. First, we ask if they want to start a group with a couple of friends. If they say yes, we give them a Small Group Starter Kit that includes:

1. A two-week starter curriculum on community from Rick Warren
2. "Helps for Host" from Rick
3. A card identifying their Community Leader
4. Tips for a successful small group
5. A copy of *Leading Small Groups with Purpose*[5]

We then follow up on new groups with the use of a decision process (see figure 5.1) and welcome and follow-up emails (see below).

If they don't feel comfortable starting a small group, we help them plug into an existing group. They complete a Join a Small Group Card (see figures 5.2 and 5.3), and we use that information to help them join a group that we know is actively seeking new members. As we do this, we still encourage them to be looking for two or more friends with whom they can start a new group at the next campaign. If someone signs up online or in person to join a group, within seven days we follow up with the small group to make sure the new person has been welcomed and fits in the group and everyone is happy.

Hello [Host Name],

We are so happy that you have committed to HOSTing a small group here at Saddleback Church! God will use you in an amazing way. He specializes in using ordinary people in extraordinary ways!

My name is _____, and I am your Small Group Pastor. I would love to find a time to connect with you and hear more of your story and how I can be praying for you. Just hit reply to set up a time.

Figure 5.1

New Group Follow-Up Process

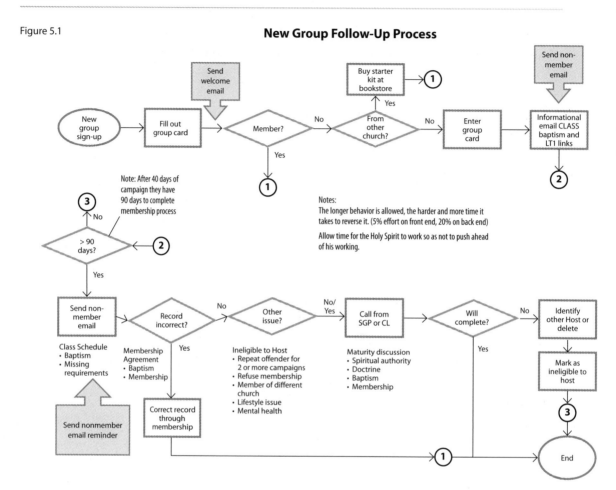

There are a few things I want to let you know as you get started HOSTing your small group.

First, Pastor Rick has said it for years, and we adopt it in our small group ministry, **we really are better together!** Of the 58 times "one another" is used in Scripture, none can be done in isolation. Check out this Scripture from Ecclesiastes 4:9–10 [ESV]: "*Two are better than one, because they have a good reward for their toil. For if they fall, one will lift up his fellow. But woe to him who is alone when he falls and has not another to lift him up.*" **We never want you to do life alone!**

Second, we want you to know that while you are HOSTing, we have teams and tools to help and support you:

- The Small Group Pastor's team (you can find us on the patio each weekend).
- Our volunteer Community Leader (CL) Team (the info for your CL is below). This CL is a trusted resource for your group's success.
- Our website for your group: www.MySaddleback.com. Beyond free curriculum, this site gives you everything you need to have a spiritually healthy group and members. **Check out the New HOST Training section designed especially for you!**

Third, our CL (community leader) Team is recruited and trained to serve you. That's their whole job! Here is a picture of the CL who will be serving you. [*Insert picture of CL, name of CL, facts about CL such as years at Saddleback, favorite movie, family.*] You can also get a ton of help at www.MySaddleback.com. Please go on it, register your group, and check out all it has to offer. Your CL will help you with all your questions about this vital group resource.

We are honored to serve you as you serve others. Thank you for following the LORD's call to lead, and please know that you are never alone!

If you need any help at all, please feel free to contact me. Your CL will be in touch with you soon.

We are praying for you and love you,

[*Small Group Pastor's name*] and the Small Groups Team

[*CL's name*] and the CL Team

Hello [*Nonmember Host Name*],

Thank you for hosting a Saddleback small group! I pray your group has been a blessing to you and your group members. In addition to continuing your small group past the recent campaign, Pastor Rick asks our small group Hosts to become Saddleback members so we can be sure we are in agreement on biblical beliefs and Saddleback's vision for our small groups. As your Spiritual Maturity Pastor,

I want to help you be the leader God wants you to be and give you the following "next step" suggestions to get you there.

Your first step is to take our Introduction to Our Church Family CLASS 101 membership class and complete the membership process. If you have already completed CLASS 101 or have questions about our membership process, please call or email Susan at (949) 609-8106, susanb@saddleback.com.

Why is church membership important? **Click here** [*link this to an appropriate website*] to learn more.

If you have not been baptized by full immersion and you are ready to take this next step, we baptize at the Saddleback Lake Forest campus after each service. Just come to the baptismal pool beside the Worship Center. We will provide shorts, shirts, and towels.

If you have additional questions about how or why we baptize, or if you have already been baptized, you can call or email Denise at (949) 609-8112, deniseb @saddleback.com to update your information. Please have the name of the church, denomination, city, state, and approximate date or year of your baptism available when you call.

Why is baptism important? **Click here** [*link this to an appropriate website*] to learn more.

Our small group HOSTs are the "frontline" of care and support for our church family; when you become a HOST, you are a leader representing Jesus Christ and Saddleback Church. That is why I want to encourage you to take the next step of becoming a member. We ask that you prayerfully consider your spiritual next steps and commit to completing our church membership process.

Will you commit to taking our Introduction to Our Church Family CLASS 101 membership class within the next 60 days? Put an X in the appropriate space below and hit "reply" to this email.

I agree to take CLASS 101. ☐ Yes ☐ No **Click here to register**. [*Link this to an appropriate website*.]

Will you commit to being baptized within the next 60 days? Put an X in the appropriate space below and hit "reply" to this email.

I agree to be baptized. ☐ Yes ☐ No

The next membership class, Introduction to Our Church Family CLASS 101, Lake Forest Campus only:

March 11, 2018	**Tent 3**	**3:00–7:30 p.m.**
April 8, 2018	**Tent 3**	**3:00–7:30 p.m.**

We will pray for you as you continue on your spiritual maturity pathway toward becoming the leader God wants you to be. Please respond to this email by [*date*]. If this email gets lost in your inbox, we'll happily send you a reminder email in the near future.

Thanks so much for HOSTing your small group, and my prayer is that you will take your next step in being a leader at Saddleback.

God Bless,

Steve Gladen

Spiritual Maturity Pastor

How Big Can a Group Get?

We at Saddleback do not subscribe to the theory that a small group needs to be kept below a maximum size. Some people are just natural gatherers. They keep inviting others until they have, perhaps, twenty or thirty people jammed into their house every Tuesday night. We don't penalize these people. Instead, we encourage groups to become any size they want and then equip them for health in ways that are appropriate to their size. We believe ratios are more important than size, and through subgrouping (see Q10 in chapter 7) we help maintain ratios of attendees to leaders at optimum levels so that participation and group health are not jeopardized. We help every group foster an environment for a life-changing, healthy community.

We encourage groups to become any size they want.

Figure 5.2

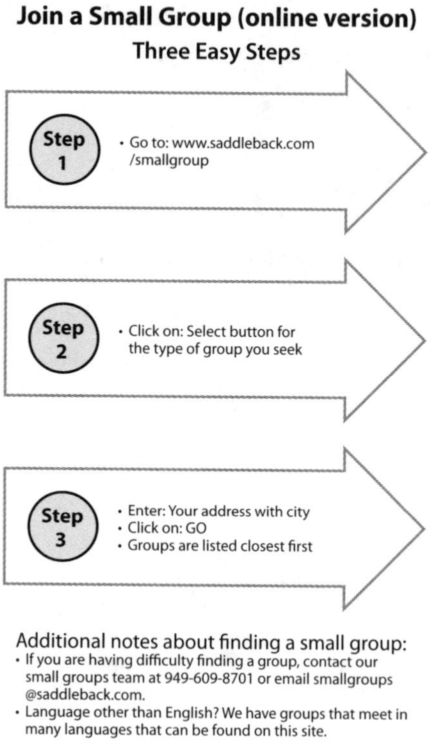

Join a Small Group (online version)
Three Easy Steps

Step 1
• Go to: www.saddleback.com
/smallgroup

Step 2
• Click on: Select button for
the type of group you seek

Step 3
• Enter: Your address with city
• Click on: GO
• Groups are listed closest first

Additional notes about finding a small group:
• If you are having difficulty finding a group, contact our
small groups team at 949-609-8701 or email smallgroups
@saddleback.com.
• Language other than English? We have groups that meet in
many languages that can be found on this site.

Three Strategies for Connecting People

There are pros and cons to every system, and you should never choose one or the other because "that is the way we've always done it." Take some time and give thought to your desired result, and then choose the delivery system that is the most effective in achieving that result.

Here are three strategies for connecting people into small groups: adult Sunday school strategy, connection event strategy, and campaign strategy.

Adult Sunday School Strategy

Adult Sunday school and small groups can coexist as long as they are aligned together and not competing with each other. There's also potential for unhealthy competition with men's, women's, couples', and singles'

Figure 5.3

Join a Small Group (paper version)

My campus: _____

Language (if not English): _____

First name: _____

Last name: _____

My home address: _____# _____

City: _____ State: _____ Zip: _____

Please use above address as my mailing address ☐

Email: _____ ☐ NEW

Birthdate: _____

Best phone number to reach me: _____

_____ ☐ cell ☐ home ☐ work

Preferred marital group type:

☐ Single ☐ Married ☐ Combined married and single

Preferred gender group type:

☐ Men ☐ Women ☐ Combined men and women

Age Group (*check only the box that best represents your group preference*):

☐ College ☐ 20s ☐ 30s ☐ 40s ☐ 50s ☐ 60s ☐ Mixed ages

Meeting Day (*day of week, all, or any*): _____

ministries if not aligned with your church's delivery systems to create healthy followers of Christ. So make sure all church ministries serve each other and the church's vision, mission, and strategy rather than building walls.

How can you start or help a healthy Sunday school ministry? Here are some practical steps:

1. Strategically set up your room. Instead of chairs in rows, seat members around tables to encourage eye contact and conversation. Or set chairs in small circles or horseshoes (open end toward the front).

2. Build consistency at each table. Encourage class members to sit in the same spot each week so they can become better acquainted with the same people. Encourage clusters of new joiners to start new tables. Mixing people every week makes members feel unsafe and discourages transparency.

3. Understand ratios. If one of your goals is to know the spiritual health of each class member and encourage personalized next steps of growth, one person can't realistically know and follow up on more than ten individuals. If your class is larger than ten, start identifying table leaders who can help you build health into each individual.

4. Set the table for evangelism. If your tables (or circles) seat eight, assign five or six people per table and ask them to invite others to fill the extra seats. Also, smaller groups encourage organic attendance accountability because a person's absence is more readily noticed.

5. Guide everyone through spiritual health assessment and planning (using something like Saddleback's Spiritual Health Assessment and Spiritual Health Planner at www.smallgroups.net/store). Assessment helps members discover where they're doing well and areas for spiritual growth. Planning helps them choose and pursue next steps into health.

6. Build spiritual accountability. Have members pair up in partnerships, regularly asking each other how they're progressing toward their personal goals. Checkups should be done as a natural part of the relationships. The teacher and table leaders don't need to know everyone's growth goals, just that everyone has a support partner.

7. Share ownership. Delegate responsibility to individuals according to their strengths in the five biblical purposes (fellowship, discipleship, ministry, evangelism, and worship). Someone at a table who is strong in fellowship may track birthdays and anniversaries or help plan a class social event. Someone strong in discipleship may oversee the Spiritual Health Assessment and Spiritual Health Plan for the people at his or her table. The strong in one area can help the weak in that area.

8. Be creative with limits. Recognize what you can do in the class time and what needs to be done outside. Generally, a Sunday school hour only permits discipleship. You can attempt fellowship, and occasionally worship. But don't attempt to accomplish all five purposes in one Sunday school hour. Encourage tables or clusters of tables to coordinate addressing some purposes outside of class. Release your people to develop themselves. If you try to contain all growth experiences within the classroom, you will limit creativity and suppress the Holy Spirit.

9. Think transformation, not just information. Sunday school originally started in England to teach children literacy on Sundays because they worked in factories five or six days per week. Over time biblical teaching was added, and even later the secular teachings were dropped as labor laws and free education fostered literacy elsewhere. That explains today's emphasis on teaching, which made perfect sense in the original context. Now Sunday schools are moving toward a missing piece of discipleship or spiritual formation: application. It's important to present information in such a way that students take the teaching with them and apply it to their lives outside the classroom.

10. Use the power of discussion. Discussion encourages members to talk through the biblical teachings, share how well they are living it, learn from each other, and encourage each other toward life change. This encourages accountability to follow through on personal growth plans. The teacher's greatest challenge is finding and

allowing discussion time. I encourage 40 percent teaching and 60 percent discussion.

The benefits of a Sunday school strategy to start groups are:

- Convenient meeting time (before or after worship)
- Child care provided
- Ease of leader management

The cons of using a Sunday school strategy to start groups are:

- Time constraints limit fellowship
- Unchurched less likely to come to a church than a home
- Limited to the number of classrooms available

Connection Event Strategy

This was our primary way to draw people into groups until we came up with the campaign strategy in 2002. It proved successful, and you may want to try it. It's now our secondary means of connecting people into groups.

We hold a two-hour connection event on campus, targeting church attendees who aren't yet connected to a small group. We recruit them through pulpit announcements, email invitations, flyers, videos, and personal invitations. All you need is a room with round tables. Depending on the size of your church, you may mark tables for singles, couples, men only, or women only. Or you may divide the room according to geography. Once people are all seated, help them get acquainted by passing out lists of questions to discuss at their tables that focus on affinity, group experience, and spiritual journey.

- What is your name?
- Where do you live?
- What are your hobbies or interests?

- Briefly (about two minutes) tell us about your spiritual journey to this point.
- How did you start attending this church, and what do you like best about it?
- What is your previous small group experience?
- What is one thing you hope to gain by being in a small group?
- What is one fear you have about joining a small group?

We allow about an hour for them to get acquainted through these questions. Then we guide them through choosing a leader using new questions for them to think about:

- Who in this group is most likely to lead?
- Who has spiritual maturity and a growing heart for God?
- Who has the most small group or ministry experience?
- Whom would you be willing to follow for six weeks?

We then ask them to close their eyes and, on the count of three, point to the person they think would make the best leader. When they are all pointing, we instruct them to open their eyes and see who has the majority of people pointing to him or her. Then—and this is critical—we ask each person to explain their selection. Then we ask the tentative leader whether he or she is willing to lead the group, using a six-week DVD curriculum (our 40 Days of Purpose curriculum at https://store.pastors.com/pages /small-group). In my years at Saddleback we have never had the chosen person say no to leading for six weeks. We provide a link for training, a curriculum, and a Community Leader to guide our new leader along his or her journey.

If you already have leaders looking for new members, you can begin the event seating them at empty tables, some perhaps choosing certain types of members (women, singles, and so on). New people join a table, bond with that leader and each other, and leave as a group.

The benefits of a connection strategy to start groups are:

- Greater sense of group ownership by members
- Curriculum and training resources immediately available
- Quick connection with Community Leaders, especially if they attend

The cons of a connection strategy to start groups are:

- May kill evangelism by replacing church attendees' existing friends with new churched friends
- Some less-than-ideal group fits because the strategy uses a degree of randomness
- More real-time customer service for people who might be at a table that isn't going well

For instructions for a connection event, see www.SmallGroups.net/connection.

Campaign Strategy

Saddleback Church was the first church to successfully use the campaign strategy. A campaign is forty days of intensive, churchwide focus on a particular aspect of spiritual growth for each age group. It encompasses weekend sermons, small group curriculum, children's activities, student ministry programs, social media, and more. One goal of our campaigns is to start new small groups.

Campaigns grew out of Rick's challenge to pray and work toward exponential group growth (see the "Exponential Thinking" section on pages 114–15). We needed a new strategy to accomplish the numbers he had in mind. This was also when we came up with the Host role, which is the only way we've found to initiate large numbers of new groups out of a campaign. As part of the campaign we ask the congregation, "If our church has ministered to you, would you in turn minister to your community and be willing to Host a small group for six weeks? All you need is two friends to start a group!" (See pages 137–39 for more on starting groups with two friends.) The first time we did this, response was overwhelming, and suddenly we had plenty of people willing to initiate new groups and lead them for the short term.

Some of these groups don't continue beyond their initial six-week commitment. But that's not reason for discouragement. Healthy groups will stay in place, growing the ministry beyond where it was. After one of our campaigns, we looked in depth at the reasons groups discontinued and found it was not because they didn't have a good experience. It was because life got in the way, and our leader coaching infrastructure wasn't in place to support Hosts. We reevaluated our infrastructure, and two years later, after our next campaign, our retention rate went from 68 percent to 86 percent.

We learned by stepping out in faith and attempting the seemingly impossible. We moved ahead before we had all the details ironed out, and we made some mistakes. But we learned from them and moved forward. Saddleback's campaign resources are available at www.store.pastors.com /pages/campaign-central so you can avoid some of our mistakes.

I'm now a multidecade veteran of campaigns at Saddleback, and I've discovered that a strategy is only as good as the foundation and follow-through. To ensure a positive outcome, check out my battle-tested tips:

1. Choose a compelling question, such as "What on earth am I here for?" (from our 40 Days of Purpose campaign), to motivate people to join small groups.

2. Align children, student, and adult ministries. This encourages natural discussions at home among all family members. It also emphasizes the importance of every church member, not just adults.

3. Stick to the principles, and apply your own methodologies. Keep the content consistent, but tailor it to each age level.

4. Language matters. We had trouble getting leaders when we called them shepherd leaders or small group leaders. People were intimidated by the term *leader*, but *Host* led to much higher participation.

5. Employ various avenues of learning, such as weekend services, discussion groups, Scripture memorization, curriculum, and ministry projects.

6. Once a year is enough. Too much of a good thing isn't a good thing and runs the risk of burning out volunteers and the congregation.

7. Provide clear start and end dates. Then people are more likely to come along for the ride.

8. Expect high intensity for staff, volunteers, and members. But allow them time to recover and process the experience at the end.

9. Remember and celebrate! Don't forget to celebrate a job well done, perhaps through an appreciation event.

10. Prepare your leader support infrastructure in advance, and give new groups a next step to increase retention rate after their short-term commitment. A good leadership principle is to make sure people sign up for their next step in the midst of the current step.

11. Give people an out at the campaign's conclusion. Of course we want groups to continue, but if the group isn't right or the stage of life doesn't allow, we don't want to cause unnecessary guilt. We want them to come back to group life when circumstances change.

12. Budget to avoid financial obstacles for people. We don't charge participants for anything in a campaign. This is an investment that pays off, it shows people we care, and it avoids roadblocks for Hosts or groups.

The benefits of a campaign strategy to start groups are:

- Low leadership bar for Hosts to lead for exponential group launch
- Hosts fill groups with their friends; high evangelism
- Whole-church alignment, children, students, and adults

The cons of a campaign strategy to start groups are:

- Taxing on staff and volunteers to coordinate forty-day campaign
- When groups start through friendships, some members feel pressured to stay when they should be free to leave

Other Stimuli for New Groups

Some good times for starting groups are *seasonal*. Aside from an annual campaign, examine the natural rhythms of your church and culture, then build group launches around the times that make the most sense.

Struggles are a second type of group-starting stimulus. Many Saddleback groups have launched out of painful times. Celebrate Recovery and support groups typically start out of ministries other than our small group ministry. The worse people's trauma, the more we want them to focus on healing through a specialized healing ministry, while they depend mostly on weekend services for other aspects of connection to the body. If they join a standard small group before they've healed, that group can turn into a support or recovery group without realizing it, and that leads to imbalance in the group's achievement of the five biblical purposes. But if one of the specialized healing groups succeeds and its members become healthy, we then want them to join or become a standard balanced small group.

Third, you can also add new groups through *significant events*. We host men's and women's events with great regularity at Saddleback, and out of these come new groups. Other significant events may target families with new babies or teens or empty nesters. You are limited only by your creativity and the life events of the people in your church.

A fourth way groups may form is through *spiritual steps*. Groups can be launched out of any spiritual step in a person's life. Some may be new believer classes, baptism classes, mission trips, or groups forming from other short-term classes.

Please Remember . . .

The great thing is, no matter what strategy you use, it is a win-win. The goal is to get people connected!

Keep in mind a couple of things. First, regardless of your strategy, it needs to be scalable. In other words, set up a strategy that will still be workable and adaptable as your ministry grows. For example, if your small group ministry expands, make sure its financial demand won't break the church. Whatever it requires on a small scale must also be affordable on a larger scale.

Second, if your church adopts the five biblical purposes for small groups, keep your groups intentional on serving, evangelism, and worship—the purposes most often neglected—not just on fellowship (relationships) and discipleship (learning). Traditional adult Sunday school tends to focus on discipleship, but it's great for getting church attendees initially connected in some way. Small groups, if not kept on target, will tend to focus exclusively on fellowship. You and all of your leaders must work hard to balance all five purposes in your small groups.

Exponential Thinking

When you add a zero to the end of your goal, you have to think differently.

Exponential thinking takes your goal and adds a God-size faith zero to the end of it. Pastor Rick Warren has a whole Leadership Lifter on this topic at www.pastors.com, but let me summarize it for you. Back before we started churchwide campaigns, Rick challenged us with the concept of exponential thinking. The previous fall's three hundred new groups had marked a banner year. But Rick said we needed to add a zero to our next year's goal—three thousand new groups!

After I woke up from passing out, some amazing things took place. First, although Rick was directing the challenge to me, it was our entire church leadership team and staff who took on the goal. We were truly better together. Second, we were free to dream and to destroy any obstacle in our way. And most important, Rick paved the way for resources and alignment across the church so we could work together. And the church-wide campaign was born.

When you add a zero to the end of your goal, you *have* to think differently. It forces you to approach the situation with fresh faith, new thinking, new creativity, and the realization that without others it doesn't stand a chance of happening. The earth-shaking part of exponential thinking isn't the goal, it's the process you go through as a team to reach the goal through faith.

I also learned that exponential thinking only applies to goal setting, not our salaries, though I made my best pitch for both.

Q3 Planning Page

Connecting People into Groups

Please see pages 86–89, "Instructions for Question Planning Pages," for how to fill this out.

Suggested Tasks		
	CRAWL	**Individual strategy:** *Create and promote a step-by-step process to get individuals—especially newcomers—connected into groups.*
	WALK	**Connection event strategy:** *Hold an event to connect the unconnected into new or existing groups.*
	RUN	**Campaign strategy:** *Pick a time on the church calendar to do a church-wide campaign to start small groups. You may use (or repeat) Saddleback's 40 Days of Purpose or 40 Days of Community.*

Your Dream	Obstacles	Actions	Timing
Long-Range (1–5 years)			
Short-Range (1–12 months)			
	Other Actions		

After you've completed this page, mark the highest-priority action for this planning question. Copy that action onto the prioritizing list, pages 221–23 in chapter 10.

How Will You Measure Your Progress?

In chapter 3 under "Saddleback's Top Ten Small Group Ministry Commitments," number three is: "I will steer clear of the numbers game." I'm not contradicting myself when I say, in a moment, that data is king. Setting definable goals with numbers is essential, as long as you're not using numbers for bragging or unhealthy competition with other churches. I like to ask, "How many, by when?" because numerical values and timing clearly define the target for everyone involved. Without them, no one knows if you succeeded. As the old saying goes, "If you aim at nothing, you'll hit it every time!"

Data Is King

Timing and numbers are important for measuring your progress. Many think it's unspiritual to talk numbers, and you are likely to meet resistance. They'll say ministry progress is all about quality, not quantity—that God doesn't care about numbers.

But that isn't true. I mean, there's even a book called Numbers in the Old Testament. It is completely possible to care about quality and quantity at the same time. The two are not mutually exclusive, nor do they need to be enemies. We count people because people count. Anticipate resistance by being prepared with your rationale, explaining how you intend to balance processes with people, because it's all for people. And it's all for eternity.

Regardless, do not be discouraged. This resistance is normal, and you can plan ahead for potential obstacles by brainstorming which obstacles may arise and planning their solutions. This will prevent others from being able to derail your great ideas and objectives.

Regarding timing, set points in time to review your progress. If you're on track, praise God! If you need to adjust course, take some time to readjust, and then start moving forward again as soon as possible.

It is completely possible to care about quality and quantity at the same time.

117

Hard and Soft Data

Hard data is the most familiar to us. This is basic contact information and church involvement—name, address, phone number, email, social media contacts, salvation date, baptism date, and metrics related to your ministry system. I think most churches do this well.

Soft data is another story. Where hard data is important to the church, soft data is important to the individual. Soft data tells his or her story. It's a window into that person's interests and priorities. A beginning, crawl step to discovering people's "soft data" stories is gathering their important calendar dates, such as family birthdays and anniversaries. An intermediate, walk step could be to learn and record people's hobbies, interests, sports involvement, and the like. A run step may be to track spiritual achievements and needs.

Soft data is important to the individual.

As you learn soft data, it is important that your church database stores this information and makes appropriate use of it to enhance relational bonds between them and key people, such as their group Hosts. When leaders gain members' trust, they can more easily challenge them to take risky steps of growth and obedience.

When hard data and soft data are both used effectively, data moves from cold, hard numbers to relationships, hearts, and stories. Furthermore, numerical goals depend in part on learning and using soft data. Appropriate use of soft data brings people in the door and helps them feel safe and supported in your church family through good times and bad.

What to Look for in Data

As you gather data, what do you do with it? Here are some questions to consider:

1. *What kinds of data are useful, and what is useless?*

   As a rule of thumb, if you're not going to use the data, don't ask for it. Basic small group data tends to focus on the number of small groups in a church and average group size. But this doesn't reflect the rich, full dynamics of healthy small groups. For instance, tracking the life spans of groups and average age of group members reveals commitment levels. But commitment doesn't guarantee health. To help measure group health and sustainability, I advise tracking such details as:

- Number of studies each group completes each year (discipleship)
- Monthly average number of social gatherings (fellowship)
- Number of service projects (ministry)
- Members' engagement in personal, local, or global outreach (evangelism)
- Group connection with the Lord through, for example, communion, prayer, or fasting (worship)

I've found one useful indicator is a Host's frequency of contact with the Community Leader. Hosts who keep in touch have the healthiest groups because they value guidance in maturing their groups. I recommend that you require leader coaches to track and report successful contacts with small group leaders compared with attempted contacts from the coach. Track indicators and measurements of spiritual health of groups and leaders.

2. *How do you obtain data?*

From my experience, the answers vary depending on the church's culture. I consider an ideal approach to be eclectic—that is, the small group ministry team partners with other church ministries to track and share data and to watch trends in various church spheres. I suggest asking small group leaders to complete a short survey about their group twice a year. There's any number of ways of gathering valuable information through websites, forms, interviews, and other sources.

But even more valuable is an honest, open relationship between small group leader and CL. Your leader support team should keep their ear to the ground and stay aware of conditions in groups and ways God is moving in the ministry.

3. *How do you respect privacy while gathering data?*

It's important to maintain your group leaders' and members' trust. Make sure their information is securely protected and that only appropriate parties access and handle it. Mentioning this on forms will help build trust.

Some small group leaders may be reluctant to share sensitive information. I make a practice of including a picture of myself and family in my introduction email to groups, and I share a short personal history and current stage of life. I consider it a requirement to avoid the Big Brother effect through personal care.

Whenever possible, requests for data should come from someone personally known to the recipient. If the needed relationships haven't yet been established, then establish them! Take every opportunity to clarify that the requested information will contribute to a healthier ministry and better care for group members.

4. *Where and how do you store and access data?*

Excel serves nicely for many churches. And several companies have designed software specifically for churches. Make sure servers, accounts, and documents are password protected. A reputable person with an IT background may be of great service in setting this up and teaching the appropriate people how to use it.

5. *How do you analyze, understand, and use data?*

These "hard facts" are details of people's lives, meant to help you understand the realities of people and groups in order to better care for them. Accurate analysis of valid data will guide you in making better ministry decisions. Some data can actually be misleading if the person using it doesn't have the story of the people behind the reports. For instance, the fact that Saddleback's recorded average group size is four people hides the reality that many Hosts don't keep their rosters updated.

Accurate analysis of valid data will guide you in making better ministry decisions.

We depend heavily on Community Leaders keeping group rosters up-to-date through their conversations with Hosts. But beyond merely deleting names, they ask why members left or groups stopped meeting, trying to get to the less visible meaning beneath the numbers.

When you are considering data conversations with people, it is important that they see your heart, and that although we have one eye on people concerning data, our other eye is on their eternity.

Q4 Planning Page

Measure Progress

Please see pages 86–89, "Instructions for Question Planning Pages," for how to fill this out.

	Suggested Tasks		
	CRAWL	**Track leaders:** *Track small group leaders with a spreadsheet (like Excel).*
	WALK	**Track members:** *Track small group leaders and individual members to know who is connected and who is not.*
	RUN	**Track development:** *Track the details of groups, such as the developmental next steps individuals and groups are taking or roles of responsibility members are fulfilling.*

Your Dream	Obstacles	Actions	Timing
Long-Range (1–5 years)			
Short-Range (1–12 months)			
	Other Actions		

After you've completed this page, mark the highest-priority action for this planning question. Copy that action onto the prioritizing list, pages 221–23 in chapter 10.

6

The Family Room

GROWING PEOPLE IN SMALL GROUPS

Q5—How Will You Define and Develop Mature Disciples?

Q6—What Outcomes Do You Want from Small Group Life?

Q7—How Will You Develop Leaders for Your Ministry?

Q8—What Support Resources Will Your Small Group Leaders Need?

This is where your job as a shepherd comes into play. You must be intentional in defining the pathways for people through your ministry and making sure your sheep find that path and know where they are headed. If you don't have a clearly defined growth and ministry path, you run the risk that your sheep will wander around aimlessly. Then all your work setting up your ministry and connecting people into small groups will be for naught.

How Will You Define and Develop Mature Disciples?

If you don't know where you are headed, how will you or anyone in your church get there? Better yet, where is "there"? If you don't know the end destination, how can you train, build tools for, provide curriculum for, guide, or coach your people? Each question in this phase will help you resolve these questions so you can have clarity in your church.

What Is Success for Jesus's Disciples?

In his Great Commission, Jesus commanded us to make disciples. If we're going to fulfill this task in our churches—particularly in your small group ministry—we need to understand what we're making. What is a mature disciple? I suggest that a mature disciple is one who succeeds in balancing the Great Commission and great commandment in his or her heart (see figure 6.1).

Figure 6.1

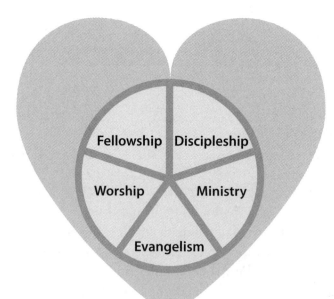

For us at Saddleback, a successful, mature disciple understands and lives out his or her God-given purpose. In some respects that purpose is unique to the individual, but the aspects that are common to every disciple come from the Great Commission and the great commandment: fellowship, discipleship, ministry, evangelism, and worship. We shape all aspects of our church efforts toward these five purposes, and we also guide small groups to target all five of these purposes. These are five key components of the definition of a successful, mature disciple.

Your model may be different, but your church needs to define success for a mature disciple. Understanding that no one on earth is perfect in the sense of being flawless, ask yourself, "If I had the 'perfect' disciple sitting next to me, what would that person do? What would he or she be? What would come out of the person's life on this earth?" If your church hasn't derived a definition of a mature disciple, here are some steps you may take:

1. With your senior pastor, choose who will work together on the definition.

2. Do a study of Jesus's earthly life—what he did and said.

3. Do a study of Jesus's prayers. What did he pray for?

4. Brainstorm answers together and write down *every* idea.

5. Cluster those ideas under attributes they describe.

6. Distill this down to major themes.

7. Craft a one-sentence definition everyone can remember.

This definition should be the tip of the spear for everything your church does, because this is what you're trying to create in every person. Every ministry, program, training, tool, and emphasis will point people to this. When a church wants to start a small group ministry, this is where I take them, because a clear statement of your target guides where you go.

Buy What You Sell

Not only do mature disciples succeed by your definition—they also model success. They live out the Christlike life in a way that influences others to do the same. At Saddleback we encourage all small group leaders and members to use our Spiritual Health Assessment and Spiritual Health Planner every year as a spiritual temperature check, in keeping with 2 Corinthians 13:5: "Test yourself to make sure you are solid in the faith. Don't drift along taking everything for granted. Give yourself regular checkups. . . . Test it out. If you fail the test, do something about it" (MSG).

Other good assessment and planning tools are available. It's important to use something to keep people taking growth steps in relational accountability. At www.SmallGroups.net/store you can get the electronic version of our assessment and planner and modify them to fit your definition of a successful, mature disciple.

Keep encouraging your entire leadership team to model maturity and continued growth and to challenge their group members to do the same, thus leading by example.

We Are Better Together

God made us so that we need each other. One way to develop mature disciples is through spiritual partners in the small group community. I suggest that a worthwhile goal is to see that each small group member has a spiritual partner. This ensures there is a go-to person and that no one ever has to stand alone. We are better together! As I've said, isolation is a powerful tool that Satan uses to derail the Christian. A partner often makes the difference.

> Two are better than one,
>   because they have a good return for their labor:
> If either of them falls down,
>   one can help the other up.

But pity anyone who falls
    and has no one to help them up.
Also, if two lie down together, they will keep warm.
    But how can one keep warm alone?
Though one may be overpowered,
    two can defend themselves.
A cord of three strands is not quickly broken. (Eccles. 4:9–12)

Who will help you stand? Whom will you help?

Define and Develop Mature Disciples

Please see pages 86–89, "Instructions for Question Planning Pages," for how to fill this out.

Suggested Tasks		
CRAWL	**Define**: *Define (with church leadership) what mature disciples are, the attributes they exhibit, the things they do.*
WALK	**Develop**: *Create your version of a Spiritual Health Assessment and Planner, and start using it with your small group leaders.*
RUN	**Distribute**: *Learn from your tool's use with leaders, get feedback about it, improve it as appropriate, and roll out your assessment and planner to everyone in small groups.*

Your Dream	Obstacles	Actions	Timing
Long-Range (1–5 years)			
Short-Range (1–12 months)			
	Other Actions		

After you've completed this page, mark the highest-priority action for this planning question. Copy that action onto the prioritizing list, pages 221–23 in chapter 10.

What Outcomes Do You Want from Small Group Life?

A small group can't accomplish its part in developing mature disciples solely through the two hours per week that the group meets. That's why I speak in terms of outcomes from "small group life," not just from small group meetings. Group members can do so much more to help each other mature during the other 166 hours each week.

Since the purpose of your small groups is to produce mature disciples, your selection of desired outcomes from your small groups is guided by your definition of a mature disciple. Whatever you want a disciple to become, that's what your small groups should produce. So, for example, at Saddleback we want the outcomes of our small groups to be fellowship, discipleship, ministry, evangelism, and worship in the lives of group members. In other words, we want small groups to help people fulfill Jesus's Great Commission and great commandment. The outcomes you target in your groups should be guided by the type of mature disciple you hope to produce.

I like to think of the outcomes of small group life in terms of *balance*, *becoming*, and *being*.

Bringing Balance to Small Group Life

A healthy group balances its life by placing emphasis on all aspects of a mature disciple. For example, at Saddleback we strive to etch the Great Commission and the great commandment on the hearts of each group member, so our group activities target all five biblical purposes:

1. *Fellowship*. Are the members of your small groups getting along well? Do they have fun at the meetings? Is there usually lots of laughter and good food? If so, fellowship is happening, right? Not necessarily. *Surface fellowship* is nothing more than hanging out and having a good time. *True fellowship*, however, dives below the surface image that people present to the world. True fellowship

not only connects people to each other but also connects them to Christ.

2. *Discipleship.* Doing a Bible study is just one piece of discipleship. Unfortunately, it is often the only piece that most groups accomplish. With intention and focus, however, group members can begin to look at discipleship as not only *learning* about the Word of God but also *living out* its truth in every aspect of their lives. They can begin to identify and take their spiritual next step and help others identify and take theirs.

3. *Ministry.* Small groups need to be more than just a meeting that happens every Thursday night; they should be engaged in ministry and meeting the needs of people within the body of Christ. Sometimes the ministry will take place right in your group as people walk through a crisis together. At other times group members use their unique gifts to help others in the body. (See more under Q11 and Q12.)

4. *Evangelism.* At Saddleback every small group has a mission to the world, and while we want our groups to focus on that, we also don't want them to forget the mission field in which they live: the people in their neighborhood or circles of influence with whom they interface throughout the week. A small group is a great place to prompt members to begin praying for their neighbors and friends and even planning activities designed for building bridges with those who are not yet followers of Christ. Evangelism can happen personally, locally, and globally (see chapter 8).

5. *Worship.* At Saddleback we work at cultivating times of worship in our small groups during which we focus on God's presence and express our love through song, prayer, praise, and other experiences. At the heart of worship is surrender, and small groups can help people live as living sacrifices. Romans 12:1 says, "I urge you, brothers and sisters, in view of God's mercy, to offer your bodies as a living sacrifice, holy and pleasing to God—this is your true and proper worship." Group life encourages transparency among members as

they receive the support they need to succeed in their Christian walk. This increased transparency provides the fertile ground for worship. (See more under Q20.)

Each group will do this a little differently, but the outcome we want in all groups is people growing together toward God. Since, by our definition, discipleship or learning is part of a mature disciple, we always put some emphasis on diving into God's Word, learning from it and from each other. Our groups also spend time each week sharing prayer requests and praises, listening to each other's answered prayers and personal victories. And since group life extends beyond the meeting, we urge members to pray for and with each other throughout the week.

Since ministry is part of our definition of a mature disciple, we expect group members to minister to each other, building into each other, helping each other toward maturity. Spiritual formation is different for each member, so what each person needs from the rest of the group varies. But when all parts of Christ's body fulfill their individual functions in each other's lives, this builds unbreakable bonds by which we carry each other through whatever life tosses into the mix.

We don't expect the leaders alone to accomplish all five biblical purposes to produce mature disciples. Everyone in the group must contribute to balanced group life. Each member's contribution will gravitate toward one part of the Great Commission or the great commandment. It is part of the leader's job to help each person find the area in which he or she is a "ten"—that is, that individual's spiritual gifting. Then capitalize on that!

Not only will this meet the practical and spiritual needs of other members, but the contributor will feel valued because he or she is making a difference, fulfilling a purpose. People have a felt need to feel needed. Some members can find fulfillment in simply bringing drinks. Or this may be a starting place for someone new or timid. You can also make use of members' contributions to solve group problems. If someone is chronically late, consider moving the meetings to his or her house.

Each member's contribution will gravitate toward one part of the Great Commission or the great commandment.

We'll talk more about distributing responsibilities among group members in chapter 7.

Helping Disciples *Become* Who God Sees Them to Be

Your definition of a mature disciple determines what you want each group member to *become*. That process of *becoming* will feel risky to the group member, requiring him or her to grow in faith by steps—sometimes baby steps. How can group members help each other through the frightening process of becoming who God sees each disciple to be? (See figure 6.2.)

Figure 6.2

Let's say a group member comes to an opportunity to do something new and risky. The devil wants to paralyze believers with fear, while Jesus wants to let them step out in faith and take the risk. The group leader or fellow group member might encourage this person to start small, in keeping with the crawl-walk-run progression I've described earlier. A crawl-level risk is easier to accept and more likely to ensure success. When the growing disciple takes that small step and succeeds, this strengthens his or her faith. Then that person is better prepared for the next opportunity, more likely to overcome fear and take a new risk.

Parents do this with children all the time. And God does it with his children. David, a man after God's heart, started tending sheep and found himself defending his flock from a lion. David killed the lion, and along came a bear. David handled the bear, and then came Goliath.

Step-by-step David's faith increased, preparing him for larger, riskier acts of faith. This is how God graduated David from tending sheep to tending the nation of Israel (see Ps. 78:70–72). And this is the developmental process by which Jesus's followers grow into mature disciples in a healthy small group.

So how can this work in your group? Everyone wants to succeed, but even the most successful people can be intimidated when facing a spiritual growth opportunity. The Bible gives us a variety of ways to help each other move forward toward Christlike outcomes:

- *Encouraging.* "You can do it. God will help you."
- *Challenging.* Start with crawling before walking or running. "Don't give up. Don't believe the lies you've been told about your limitations. Take the next step."
- *Supporting.* Stand alongside; find strength in numbers and prayer.
- *Equipping.* Teaching, training, and giving the knowledge, skills, and experience people don't yet have.

Keep finding or developing tools your small group members can use to become mature disciples. You can find ideas in *Leading Small Groups with Purpose*, *250 Big Ideas*, and *Don't Lead Alone*, all available at www .SmallGroups.net/store. Adapt these ideas or create your own to help leaders and members become who God designed them to be.

Helping Disciples Consistently *Be* Who They Are

When life doesn't go according to plan, *being* helps group members remain steadfast and trust God in spite of the circumstances. At Saddleback we use our CLASS system (specifically CLASS 201) to show people how to start being a Christian built on a firm foundation. We teach them to slay the common Orange County giants of busyness, materialism, and isolation, which are enemies of *being*. We also make this available in a small group curriculum. This is a starting point for groups to focus away from "me" and toward "being in Christ," secure and rock solid. What is your church's starting point to anchor *being* in your people?

At www.SmallGroups.net/free we offer a folder with free Spiritual Growth Tools that you can download and adapt for your church. These take people beyond the first stage of *being*. These and other such tools can be used in groups, but most of our groups let their members work on personalized growth steps outside group meetings.

Again, each group will look different, but as practices that encourage steadfast *being* in members, we urge all of our groups to spend time every week sharing prayer requests and praises and then praying for each other. We also encourage members to keep communicating and praying for each other through the week. And, of course, the learning component in groups is important to keep them continually abiding in Christ and his Word, learning from it and each other.

Curriculum

What your small groups study is one of the most important choices to ensure that your small groups accomplish your church's end purpose—to grow mature disciples. At Saddleback Church we use video curriculum that has been developed to help group members accomplish the Great Commission and the great commandment in a balanced way. The individual curriculum study series are categorized according to which of the five biblical purposes it builds—fellowship, discipleship, ministry, evangelism, or worship.

We provide a curriculum pathway that our small group leaders can follow in choosing their group's course of study. Not every group follows this curriculum exactly, but it provides important guidance for those who need it. (See appendix.) New groups are especially prone to "curriculum paralysis," so we offer only two choices for young groups to help avoid indecision.

Many churches believe they can't afford to produce video curriculum. But one thing I have learned is that church attendees love to hear from their shepherd and are forgiving if quality is lacking. Even on a limited budget, it is easy to produce video curriculum for groups that supports your church's system and purpose. Today's smartphones produce video quality that is good enough for this purpose. All you need is one of your teaching pastor's old sermon series from which you can develop twenty-minute video clips. To guide group discussion, all you need are three or four questions—an opening question, a couple of questions to process the teaching, and an application question.

Q6 Planning Page

Outcomes from Small Group Life

Please see pages 86–89, "Instructions for Question Planning Pages," for how to fill this out.

Suggested Tasks		
CRAWL	**Balance**: *Teach your small groups to spend time serving together outside their weekly meeting.*	
WALK	**Becoming**: *Ask small group leaders to write down a suggested next spiritual step for each of their members, and coach leaders in the art of gently guiding members to take their next steps.*	
RUN	**Curriculum**: *Develop a curriculum pathway that supports your small group vision and mission.*	

Your Dream	Obstacles	Actions	Timing
Long-Range (1–5 years)			
Short-Range (1–12 months)			
	Other Actions		

After you've completed this page, mark the highest-priority action for this planning question. Copy that action onto the prioritizing list, pages 221–23 in chapter 10.

How Will You Develop Leaders for Your Ministry?

When I am speaking with small group point people or at conferences, the number one question that comes up is how to find enough small group leaders at your church, which then leads to how to develop and train said leaders. But is the issue not having enough leaders at your church? Or is the problem the process we use?

Jesus's Low Bar for Leadership

At the center of Saddleback's philosophy are two principles. First, we model our leader development after the way Jesus recruited and developed his disciples. Jesus's first requirement to be a disciple was "follow me" (Matt. 4:19). Three years later the disciples were willing to die for Jesus. In the New Testament you see Jesus grow his disciples from a come-and-see mentality to a come-and-die mentality. He took them through a process. He didn't water down his expectations, but he had a plan in place. Our Small Group Leadership Development Pathway seeks to do the same thing—to take Hosts from "come and see" to "come and die." Now we hope this never means physical death, but dying spiritually to self, time, and finances in order to do Jesus's kingdom work!

Two Friends

Since we have in place guardrails to protect against abuses, we take anyone who has at least two friends and start a group with our video curriculum. You see, the foundation for leadership is followers. The modern term for followers is *friends*. For us the minimal starting point for leadership is, "Do you have two friends?" If you think you are a leader and do not have followers, you are just taking a walk. We have would-be leaders who want the church to fill their small group. But we will say, "You want to lead a group? Great! Grab two of your friends and start a group." The would-be leaders react one of two ways: Either they grab

If you think you are a leader and do not have followers, you are just taking a walk.

two friends and start a group or they ask to be placed in a small group as followers.

Now I know what you are thinking. What if someone who attends my church isn't a Christian and wants to start a group with two friends? Well first, that person's friends are also probably not followers of Christ. If this group meets and follows our video curriculum, the unbelieving are evangelized! Second, I don't believe these people are starting sleeper cells to destroy our church. They like our church. And third, some would say these groups are destroying the moral fabric of our church. But suppose a group of nonbelievers visited your weekend service and afterward discussed the message. Would you endorse their gathering and discussing the sermon? I am sure 100 percent of you would say *yes*! That's what we have—nonbelievers grabbing a couple of friends, watching our video curriculum, and discussing it. In fact, we keep in close touch with them. When they pick up the free starter curriculum or campaign curriculum, we gather their contact information and introduce them to a Community Leader, who then follows up and gets to know them. The Community Leader's first job is to discover whether they need Christ or they need training for longer-term leadership.

We also have other safeguards. For example, a search for small groups on our website doesn't turn up a particular group until its leaders are church members.

The benefits of starting groups organically through friendships are:

1. No awkwardness going to a stranger's home. Friends have already been there.
2. No scheduling problems, because friends already get together, and now existing friendships can go deeper with purpose.
3. No problems working around summer and holidays, because friends love getting together during these times.

For selecting small group leaders, your church leadership will need to decide the methods that are most appropriate and fruitful for your

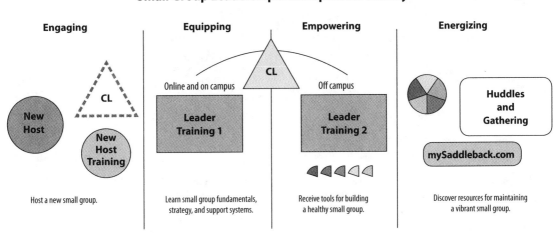

Small Group Leadership Development Pathway Figure 6.3

church. What I've described is the latest we have found to work for Saddleback.

A Pathway for Growing Leaders

You also need a pathway for developing leaders. As an example, I describe Saddleback's Small Group Leadership Development Pathway in figure 6.3.

The goal of this pathway is to develop our Hosts ultimately into leaders who are spiritually strong and godly and who are growing their group to new levels of vibrancy. The pathway involves four phases: *engaging, equipping, empowering,* and *energizing,* each calling for greater commitment to the call of Christ.

Engaging Our Leaders

First, we need to *engage* our leaders, starting where they are now in their spiritual journey. We begin this immediately when a new Host signs up. As I've explained, we start many small groups through campaigns, inviting people to sign up as new Hosts and starting groups with two or

139

more friends for about a six-week commitment. Then we assign the new group to a Community Leader (CL). Whenever possible, these assignments are determined by existing relationships, connecting new Hosts to a CL who already knows them. After that we consider geography and other factors.

The new Host receives an email introducing the CL as well as providing information about the numerous available training videos. After the initial contact, our CL follows up with a series of three phone calls. He or she calls before the first small group meeting to pray for and encourage the new Host. Then the CL calls after the first meeting to see how everything went and to offer tips and tools or whatever else the Host may need. The third call comes around the third to fourth week to check in, help the Host choose the group's next curriculum, and remind the Host that the CL is available for any needs as the small group matures.

In reality, some groups continue and some don't, which is part of life. If a group continues on, the CL has an established relationship to guide the Host to the next phase of leadership. If a group doesn't continue, we might contact the Host's group members and ask them to consider starting their own group or plug into an existing group.

Equipping Our Leaders: Leader Training 1

Your newer leaders need basic training to ensure they develop a good foundation of understanding and habits. Our *equipping* phase provides a handful of vital basics online, in a group of a few leaders, or in an on-campus class. We explain to Hosts:

- How small groups fit into our church system

- Survival tips for the early stages of their group's development

- Introduction to spiritual health, including use of our Spiritual Health Assessment and Spiritual Health Planner

- All the systems we have in place to support Hosts

This training is broken down into modules and is offered for different learning styles, including traditional classroom, flip learning (private video viewing followed by classroom consolidation), and online training. We've discovered that only 40 percent of people prefer traditional classroom-style learning. It's imperative to adapt your methods so that all of your leaders receive the training they need for effectiveness.

Also, to ensure continuity, make sure your leaders sign up for the next phase of training before they leave at the end of their current phase.

Empowering Our Leaders: Leader Training 2

Beyond the basics, your leaders need ongoing training to hone their skills and experience. They will lead most effectively if they feel confident, and you build confidence by showing them how to lead well in your particular ministry and church setting.

We provide our Leader Training 2 off campus, in a setting and manner conducive to relationships. This walks our Hosts through the five biblical purposes—fellowship, discipleship, ministry, evangelism, and worship—in relation to the Great Commission and the great commandment. We teach them to use our Group Planner to devise a practical plan in all five purposes for their unique small group. Each modular training provides crawl, walk, and run examples and helps Hosts plan implementation in their groups. Community Leaders are encouraged to teach this portion of the pathway.

Energizing Our Leaders

All of your leaders need ongoing support and equipping. Even veteran leaders can lose perspective or settle into ruts. The only way to keep everyone on target to accomplish your ministry's vision and mission is to repeat these training programs often, along with other ongoing training topics to keep leaders fresh and effective.

In Saddleback's *energizing* phase we keep working with our Hosts to ensure their groups continue to successfully balance the Great Commission and the great commandment. We do this through frequent Community Huddles and annual Leader Gatherings.

Community Huddles are groups of two or three Hosts, clustered by geography, who meet every six to eight weeks to learn from each other. We offer these Huddles in two formats. In the first format, Hosts meet for training from a Community Leader (generally highlighting modules from Leader Training 2), as well as gaining insights from each other's experience. The second format structures the time around the "Four Ps": praise, problem, plan, and pray. Each Host starts by sharing something good (praise). Then the Host tells the other leaders about any problems encountered in his or her group, and the Huddle discusses how to best handle it. Planning guides each Host's proactive intentions to ensure the small group's health. And the other Hosts commit to praying for each other between Huddles, which helps them get to know each other personally.

At Saddleback, our annual Leader Gatherings serve three primary purposes: First, we make sure they know how deeply we *appreciate* them. We give them personally written notes, recognize them publicly, or provide a tchotchke—some small gift that they'll see daily as a reminder of our appreciation. Second, Rick Warren shares our *vision* and how each leader is a crucial part of successfully executing that vision over the next year—often in preparation for an upcoming churchwide campaign. Last, we *recruit* new Hosts, asking our leaders to bring someone who may rise to leadership. This is also a good time to recruit Community Leaders.

It takes a village to raise a spiritually healthy small group.

Ongoing Leader Support

You've heard that "it takes a village to raise a child." Well, guess what? It takes a village to raise a spiritually healthy small group. Figure 6.4 illustrates the "village" and the parts we use to ensure group health. We are passionate about giving care to our leaders and offering many avenues for support. For example, our senior pastor often talks about his small group

Figure 6.4

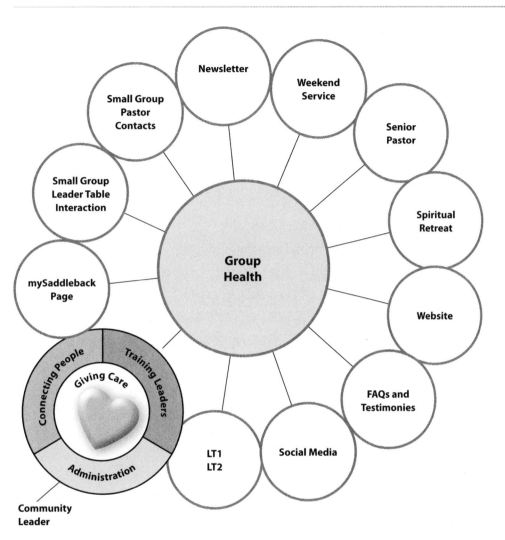

experience and preaches on relational community. Leaders take spiritual retreats to focus on God and prayerfully consider their roles.

The most crucial piece of group health is the personal touch, especially between each small group leader and his or her coach. At Saddleback we want the Host–Community Leader relationship to develop and grow, following a pattern in which the CL progresses from *friend* to *leader* to *coach*.

In the **FRIEND** stage we want the CL to:

Find common ground

Replenish the leader's soul

Invest in the leader's interests

Encourage the leader's calling

Notice the leader between meetings with calls, texts, and notes

Develop authentic relationship with the leader

In the **LEADER** stage the CL should:

Listen to the leader and help the leader improve his or her listening skills

Engage the leader in the Small Group Leadership Development Pathway

Activate the leader's personal evangelism

Develop subgrouping in the leader's small group

Enlist group members in roles of responsibility in the group

Remember to celebrate wins

In the **COACH** stage we want the CL to:

CLASSes—guide leader to attend all CLASSes

Open up next steps in leadership development

Affirm leader's personal and group plan

Curriculum—guide strategy for leader's group

Host a Community Huddle of leaders

This relationship with a CL ensures that their Hosts know they are cared for and supported and that they are also developing as leaders. This process continues to equip each generation of leaders so they too can lead healthy groups.

We train CLs for these three phases, which are described in the Community Leader Pocket Guide. We continually remind our CLs, "Before you train Hosts to be leaders, make sure they know you're their friend.

Before you coach your Hosts—challenging them in ways they never thought possible—make sure you are leading well." The relationship between CL and Host must be built on a firm foundation of trust.

As you look at your "village"—everything in your church that contributes to group health—the primary contributors are typically the senior pastor, the small group ministry point person, and the leader coaches. But all contributors are important to keep the vision and mission in front of the people, aligning the small groups with the whole church's progress toward its end purpose. Take a moment to identify your contributors, based on figure 6.4. Do your best to work toward their alignment.

As the small group ministry point person, don't allow yourself to lose touch with your small group leaders. Don't allow your mid-level leaders, such as Community Leaders, to become a barrier between you and the people in the trenches. Cheryl Bachelder, the former CEO of Popeye's Chicken, encouraged me to manage our groups through "skip leveling." She taught everyone in her organization to periodically talk to people two levels below them in order to gain their sense of the business's pulse. Brilliant! Learn to skip levels.

Develop Leaders

Please see pages 86–89, "Instructions for Question Planning Pages," for how to fill this out.

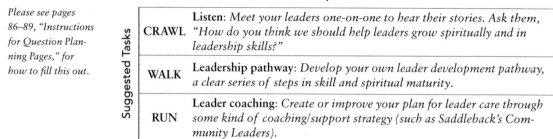

Suggested Tasks		
CRAWL	**Listen**: *Meet your leaders one-on-one to hear their stories. Ask them, "How do you think we should help leaders grow spiritually and in leadership skills?"*
WALK	**Leadership pathway**: *Develop your own leader development pathway, a clear series of steps in skill and spiritual maturity.*
RUN	**Leader coaching**: *Create or improve your plan for leader care through some kind of coaching/support strategy (such as Saddleback's Community Leaders).*

Your Dream	Obstacles	Actions	Timing
Long-Range (1–5 years)			
Short-Range (1–12 months)			
	Other Actions		

After you've completed this page, mark the highest-priority action for this planning question. Copy that action onto the prioritizing list, pages 221–23 in chapter 10.

What Support Resources Will Your Small Group Leaders Need?

The long-term success of your leaders is determined in large part by the support and resources they receive. Church budgets are notorious for providing less than you think you need. But remember that "resources" means more than money, and God will also provide wisdom to help you grow an amazing ministry with inadequate material resources.

Limitations will force creativity. One of my most creative moments came when Saddleback Church did not have the money to hire another full-time Small Group Pastor. The ministry had grown to the point where I needed help, but our budget had not yet expanded to that level. So we created the paid position of ten-hour Community Leader, which continues to play an integral role (though all Community Leaders are now volunteers). Our limited budget did not hinder our situation; instead it compelled us to be creative and ultimately enhanced and blessed our ministry beyond what we had ever dreamed.

Understand the Whole-Church Terrain

Since your ministry budget is, sometimes uncomfortably, tied in with the whole church's budget, you need to realize that *budgeting* starts long before you start crunching numbers. It begins with fostering healthy, trusting relationships with other key leaders in your church—especially the senior pastor, people with influence, and ministry leaders who may perceive you as a competitor. That's why we talked so much in chapters 1 and 4 and in Q1 about your relationship with other church leaders and ministries. In an environment of trust and mutual support you're more likely to receive both tangible and intangible resources to support your leaders.

As I've said, you need to ensure that your ministry helps fulfill the church's vision. But you can also look for ways to remind the rest of the church—especially senior and other leaders with financial influence—of your small group ministry's vision. Your small group ministry plan, which you are developing in this book, will prove useful as you communicate

The long-term success of your leaders is determined in large part by the support and resources they receive.

with others. You are clearly defining your ministry vision (your dream), your mission (your purpose), and all important supporting logistics so you can share them effectively with other church leaders.

When you talk with them about small groups, highlight the ways your ministry's vision supports and fulfills *their* vision. Sometimes it's helpful to convey your vision concisely, using a business concept called an "elevator pitch." Design a brief spoken description that can present your ministry vision accurately, concisely, and compellingly within the duration of an elevator ride.

We're talking about ways of influencing for change, but different churches change at different paces. Is your church a rowboat or an oil tanker? A rowboat can change direction in six or eight feet, but a tanker requires ten or twelve miles to turn. Be prepared for the time your church requires for change. You may encounter institutional ruts—patterns of entrenched, unchallenged thinking, sometimes harkening back to the glory days, sometimes spawned by fear of switching tracks. In this and some other aspects of budgeting, remember the wisdom of crawl-walk-run and start small.

Is your church a rowboat or an oil tanker?

Remember, you have to give in order to get. Keep thinking "whole church." Remember that your ministry functions best as part of a larger organism and that it will function poorly on its own. I'm one of the biggest small group guys on the planet, and I firmly believe in the house-to-house movement, but never at the expense of the temple courts. Every part of your church body is healthiest in the context of a healthy, *whole* church body.

Think Critically: Accomplish More with Less

Even if you have an ample ministry budget, God commissions you to steward his wealth wisely, not wastefully. And if your budget is meager, this is especially so. Before you decide how to spend your budget, pray for wisdom and seek God's guidance to use what you have economically, yet also for great eternal impact. I find this kind of critical thinking is best guided by good questions, so here are a few:

1. *What do we need to terminate?* Examine what you've done in the past that isn't working, and stop doing it. Also consider "strategic abandonment." You may be doing something that is currently effective but that needs to be abandoned to move your ministry to the next level.

2. *What can we combine?* Are there things you are doing that you can mix together to make something new and better? At Saddleback we saw the value of Alcoholics Anonymous, but we wanted something Christ-based so we created a new ministry called Celebrate Recovery. Celebrate Recovery is now in over 27,000 churches as well as prison systems across the United States.

3. *What efficiency barriers can we dismantle?* At one point we simplified our structure by eliminating a layer in our ministry between the Community Leaders and the Small Group Pastors. Another time we asked, What barriers can we remove to make our ministry more accessible? The title "Small Group Leader" was intimidating potential leaders, so we introduced the term *Host*. We never changed the requirements; we just changed the terminology and helped clarify our Hosts' next steps at each stage. We've also removed unnecessary steps to make things easier. We didn't want Saddleback to expend unnecessary energy trying to match people into groups, so we took the organic "two friends" approach (see Q7), encouraging self-starting groups. It became simple and has proven successful.

4. *What can we reincarnate?* What have we used in the past that we can bring back to life in a new form? We used to do our Spiritual Health Assessment on paper, but it was much too cumbersome to retrieve that paperwork, so it basically fell on its face. We decided to go electronic, and new life was breathed into it.

5. *What can we coordinate to make things faster, larger, and cheaper?* We use www.SmallGroup.com, which allows us to create curriculum from the temple court sermons. This also helps us combine

training for multiple ministries through the same avenues at lower expense.

6. *What are we doing that we can change, repurpose, or rejuvenate?* We did this with our Daniel Plan. We knew people would embrace the health theory behind the Daniel Plan, but we also feared it would become like many diets and fade out. We wanted to create a lifestyle, so we connected it to God's Word, and Rick did a sermon series on it. This took what we already had but worked it to the advantage of what really honors God.

7. *Are there problems we can look at in a new light?* We were having challenges getting people connected who lived far away, so we decided to utilize our online community. We have virtual groups where people first meet in a virtual environment, then later we move them into a physical environment.

8. *What can we do to make our ministry more appealing?* I encourage you to read *Creativity, Inc.* by Ed Catmull and Amy Wallace. It's a great book about Disney and how they explored various avenues in order to refine their processes. For example, based on the book's discussion of brainstorming and collaboration, we developed our "Start a Group" box, which provided a clear, uniform process for our campuses to start groups outside of campaigns.

Preparing a Budget: How to Spend

And now, finally, we come to the spending decisions. This is where many start budgeting, but if you've laid the groundwork I've described above, many of your spending decisions will make themselves, and you'll be able to provide greater support for your leaders with whatever resources God entrusts to you. Here are a few pointers:

Be a conduit, not a container.

1. Budget 10 percent to bless other church ministries. Be a conduit, not a container.

2. Earmark financial capital to build relational capital among the leaders in your ministry, your greatest asset. Provide for them in ways that show you care.

3. Budget to launch or improve an online strategy. This extends your reach exponentially.

4. Be sure to fund leadership training, leader support infrastructure, and, if it fits your model, video curriculum.

5. Discontinue extraneous advertising costs. Word of mouth is your best friend!

6. Print less, email more. Not only is this eco-friendly, but it saves money, increases efficiency, and expands your reach.

7. Use volunteers. Allow people to receive the priceless blessing of worshiping through offering God their time, energy, and abilities.

8. Itemize your budget. A more specific budget is likely to gain greater support and justification in the minds of financial decision makers.

9. Budgets often get cut. Prepare by knowing your ministry priorities and what you can afford to do with less or without.

10. To guide this year's budget decisions, look at the real experience of previous years. What did you accomplish at what cost? This removes some of the theory and replaces it with hard facts.

To maintain healthy relationships with other leaders and ministries, and to sustain their enthusiasm for your ministry, it's good practice to report regularly on what you are doing with the money you've been given. Bring them in on your celebrations of your ministry's life impact. Stories bring life!

In summary, never let limited financial resources slow you or stop you in a universe that is completely owned by your Father. Remember, for greatest effectiveness, foster and use positive relational influence, work in alignment with whole-church purpose, think critically about stewarding God's resources economically, and then make your budgeting decisions.

Resources for *You*!

Today, with the vast internet and hundreds of established churches and ministries sharing their wealth of experience, you can find an endless supply of helpful ideas and resources for your ministry. Here are some free or low-cost resources geared for the small group point person:

SmallGroups.net

You may be starting out in small group ministry as the point person or as a group leader, or you may be a veteran looking for new resources to polish your model. In any case, this website is dedicated to you—paid or volunteer, full-time or part-time. I guarantee the resources, and with over three hundred free downloads available, it will not waste your time. My prayer is that these resources will sharpen your focus, intensify your leadership skills, and aid in building healthy and balanced lives around the Great Commission and the great commandment. This website also applies to Sunday schools, cell groups, meta groups, G12 groups, Training 4 Trainers, Church Planting Movements, and house churches.

Podcast: Group Talk

The host interviews influential leaders throughout the world on relevant topics related to leading a small group ministry. The podcast is hosted on iTunes and described at www.SmallGroupNetwork.com.

Newsletter

This monthly newsletter offers tips, additional resources, and inspirational stories. Register at www.SmallGroupNetwork.com to join our newsletter distribution list.

Social Media

You can access all of our social channels at www.SmallGroupNetwork .com.

- Facebook Group: Join the conversation with thousands of other small group point people. This active group posts important questions daily.
- Twitter: Follow us and get involved!
- Instagram: Follow us and receive informative updates in a creative, fun way.
- YouTube: Subscribe to our channel and watch hundreds of videos on small group ministry point person tips, training and development, and motivational messages. On our show *SMALLer Group Talk*, I speak from my ministry experience.

Events

We offer events located across the globe to help equip, resource, and inspire small group ministry point people.

- Accelerate!: You and your team will take a 360-degree view of your small group ministry as you develop a comprehensive strategic action plan. This workshop gives you stimulating ideas, and you'll leave with a plan that you can begin to implement immediately. Attendance is limited to allow more interaction with other participants.
- Lobby Gathering: The Small Group Network is gathering only the sharpest, brightest, and most innovative small group practitioners from around the world to exchange ministry strategies, learnings, and best practices in a peer-to-peer environment.
- Small Group Conference: Need to learn the essentials for your small group ministry? This conference teaches the essentials and how to implement them.

You can register for one of our events at www.SmallGroupNetwork.com /events.

Huddles

The Small Group Network believes strongly in the importance of small group point people meeting a few times per year to share ideas, encouragement, and resources. You will find like-minded people who are experiencing the same challenges, successes, and discoveries. Huddles are located across the globe. To join or start a Huddle, visit www.Small GroupNetwork.com/huddles.

Communities of Purpose

As you develop your small group ministry plan, we have Communities of Purpose (COPs) who gather monthly to hold each other accountable in executing their plans. These are peer-to-peer learning groups held virtually or physically, depending on the COP host. Go to www.SmallGroup Network.com/cop to find the one for you.

Regional Leaders

Wherever you are around the world, we have local Regional Leaders to serve you, to help you contextualize your small group ministry to your cultural area. Go to www.SmallGroupNetwork.com/about to meet your Regional Leader.

Preparing Your Small Group Ministry Calendar

Below are some items I always track on my small group ministry calendar. I highly recommend a working calendar, especially as your ministry grows. It is so easy, and so common, to be busy to the point of forgetfulness. (Or is that just me?)

Based on the size of your small group ministry, you may schedule these weekly, monthly, quarterly, semiannually, annually, and so on.

- Leadership trainings for small group leaders and leaders at other levels
- Campaigns or the equivalent—at Saddleback an annual event that focuses the whole church on one theme

- E-newsletter, social media, group texts—useful to inform, remind, motivate, and celebrate in ways that reinforce your paradigm. What you celebrate gets replicated.

- Singles', couples', men's, women's, and workplace events—gatherings that edify people through shared affinities, also avenues for launching new small groups or recruiting people to place in groups

- Team meetings—paid staff or your ministry oversight team

- Meetings or retreats for leader coaches

- New group start-up promotions—such as sermons or cultural calendar events

- New curriculum releases—a good way to inject momentum into group life

- Small Group Appreciation Week—to honor small group leaders (we encourage group members by email to affirm their leaders in a variety of ways)

- Small group leader gatherings—corporate events for all your small group leaders to express appreciation, cast vision, and recruit (we typically have two per year, one to equip and another to encourage)

- Roster update—our version of spring cleaning, rallying small group leaders to help bring our database up-to-date

- Spiritual Health Assessment promotion—a churchwide emphasis on spiritual checkups

Icing on the Calendar Cake

- Birthdays of all leaders and other servants in your ministry (to remind you to email, text, use social media, call, or send cards)

- Bonus points: spouses' and kids' birthdays

- Anniversaries for all of the above

- Visits to as many small groups as possible (bring snacks!)

- One-on-one contact with your small group leaders (or at least with your coaches if you have a lot of groups)
- "Weekend awareness"—weeks or seasons for promoting your small group ministry (a booth or table, announcements, testimonies, and more)
- Follow-up on potential new small group leaders and members
- Efforts for gathering testimonies from your satisfied customers, perhaps through leaders or ministry overseers

Q8 Planning Page

Support Resources

Please see pages 86–89, "Instructions for Question Planning Pages," for how to fill this out.

Suggested Tasks	**CRAWL**	**Budget:** *Strategize three ways to accomplish more with less money, asking questions like those in the "Think Critically" list above.*
	WALK	**Reward:** *Give your leaders some resources to help them or their group grow spiritually—for example, an article, book, or retreat.*
	RUN	**Right hand:** *Choose someone to ask to be your right-hand, go-to person. You may not be able to pay him or her, but most likely the greatest reward is significance in making an eternal impact.*

Your Dream	Obstacles	Actions	Timing
Long-Range (1–5 years)			
Short-Range (1–12 months)			
	Other Actions		

After you've completed this page, mark the highest-priority action for this planning question. Copy that action onto the prioritizing list, pages 221–23 in chapter 10.

7

The Study

INVESTING IN GOD'S KINGDOM THROUGH SMALL GROUPS

How Will You Develop Group Members into Leaders?

I encourage you to "think developmentally" about your small group ministry. Once you have established your ministry and have a handful of groups up and running, it is important to continue investing in both leaders and their group members. This is where maturity within groups really takes off. In order to foster the relationship necessary to develop leaders, you must be able to speak truth into their lives. That privilege is built on a platform of trust, and trust is built on time. *You cannot rush this process.*

Figure 7.1

As a small group develops slowly into a family unit, existing leaders can actively work to develop other leaders within their groups.

Figure 7.1 illustrates Saddleback's progression from seeker to leader. It takes time to develop leaders because growth takes time. But we must all keep in mind our ultimate goal of moving everyone to their highest potential of maturity and ministry commitment.

Community

Small Group Ministry:	The local unconnected population in and around your church
Small Group:	Those not in your group whom you are praying to bring in

Crowd

Small Group Ministry:	Those in your church database who attend small groups
Small Group:	Those attending your small group

Congregation

Small Group Ministry:	People fulfilling roles of responsibility in small groups
Small Group:	Members fulfilling a formal or informal role in your group

Committed

Small Group Ministry:	People fulfilling the role of Host and Future Host in small groups
Small Group:	Your group's Future Host

Core

Small Group Ministry:	All small group ministry leadership teams
Small Group:	Your small group's Host

At Saddleback we add a sixth level, "Commissioned," for groups engaged in outreach through our PEACE Plan, but most churches do not engage entire small groups in large-scale outreach.

I encourage you to design a ministry in which all members are continually progressing toward their next stage of growth and commitment, never stagnating. You'll recognize natural leadership potential in some group members, while others will surprise you. Saddleback's methods may or may not translate to your situation, so you must diligently work on a plan that effectively develops group members into leaders in your unique setting.

Here are a few pointers:

1. *Prayer.* Are you and your leadership team spending meaningful time asking God to bring more people into group life so they can be transformed? Are you and your team asking God to raise up the leaders you need?

2. *Vision.* Is your vision big enough? Are the people in your ministry hearing you and others consistently talk about your vision for small groups? Are you encouraging all of them to cast the net far and wide?

3. *Goals.* Do your goals coincide with your vision? Are you and your team setting big, hairy, audacious annual goals? Goals that motivate your team to passionately recruit leaders and invite people into group life? This is risky, but it is absolutely necessary if you are going to arrive at a destination bigger than your dreams.

4. *Strategy.* Does your strategy include new ways to find leaders, train leaders, and help leaders start new groups? Ideally every trained leader will train another, who will start another group. This ripple effect creates exponential growth.

Expect All Group Members to Get Involved

Even for the many who will never wear a leader's title, you can sustain a ministrywide expectation that everyone will learn to lead others by their example and influence. For many this begins by taking simple responsibilities in their group.

At Saddleback Church we believe "every member is a minister," based in part on Ephesians 4:11–16. Not every member feels like a minister, and some will resist. But God has equipped each of us with our own set of gifts, and each one fulfills Jesus's Great Commission and great commandment by exercising those gifts in some type of service. Train your leaders to expect every member to take at least beginning baby steps into various roles of service and responsibility. Once they taste the reward of making a difference, they will naturally progress toward greater responsibilities.

Every member is a minister.

I have learned that not everyone loves titles, partly because a title creates a sense of obligation from which the person may feel there is no escape. However, people are willing to take on responsibilities or untitled roles. Train and encourage your leaders to give each group member a clearly defined task of some kind, ideally in keeping with their interests and abilities. It's important to keep each task within the person's ability to ensure that he or she succeeds in the assigned role. See figure 7.2 for some examples of roles members may fill in a small group.

The following story from Janet Collins of Lakeside Church, Guelph, Ontario, Canada, illustrates this idea in action:

> Finding a role for every person in the Small Group is so important. I put together a list of roles for my group and in my mind started slotting people into the roles I thought they would best fit. Some were already naturally taking on roles and asking to help. I began by asking these people to keep doing their tasks on a consistent basis. I did not give them an official title or role, just a task or activity they loved to do. Then I began to see roles that were not being covered, and I focused on looking for people who had gifts in those areas. People who have a passion in an area become creative, and their service enriches the group experience for everyone. Some also become motivated to serve beyond the group because they love what they do for the kingdom.
>
> Using the five areas of a healthy small group, here are some examples of ways I've encouraged people to get involved:

Worship. One man loves music. He is not a professional singer, but he relates music and lyrics to life. I asked him to bring a song to share one time during the semester. He began the very next week and continued week after week. This fueled his passion, and I never had to ask again. He began to bring printed lyrics so the group could sing along, and he prepared a reflection question.

I've also thought of inviting people to organize prayer or communion.

Fellowship. One woman asked to organize our snack schedule and potluck sign-up sheets. She in turn got others serving by bringing snacks. Another gentleman took on setting up our meeting room and making the coffee and tea.

Discipleship. I love getting people involved in coleading. One friend loves to research passages of Scripture, their cultural context, and ideas for application today. I learn so much from his teaching, and the group enjoys a richer, deeper understanding of the Bible.

Ministry. I have women who bring cards for the group to sign to support or encourage a member through some difficulty. One year two members struggled with serious health issues, and these women organized the group to bless them with cookies, poinsettias, and cards. We also assigned people to check up on them and let them know we were praying.

Another member heard about our food distribution center's need for peanut butter. She challenged the group to bring as much as they could, scouted store sales, counted donations, and announced the results.

Evangelism. One person got everyone to bring gifts for Operation Christmas Child, organized a potluck for people to assemble gift shoe boxes, and coordinated people to deliver them. When my neighbor broke his elbow and couldn't work, one woman cooked meals, which I delivered. The rest prayed for him and for my outreach to him. This opened the door for my husband and me to get to know him and care for him in a practical, unexpected, no-strings-attached way.

When people have a role in the group, they feel valued and affirmed, and everyone benefits. These people take ownership of the group.

Rick Warren taught me, "People don't do what you merely expect, people do what you inspect." Build into your strategy some way of inspecting

People don't do what you merely expect, people do what you inspect.

Small Group Roles and Responsibilities

Figure 7.2

Future Host

Purpose: To serve the group Host and regularly rotate leadership.

"The things which you have heard from me . . . entrust these to faithful men who will be able to teach others also." 2 Timothy 2:2 NASB

Primary Function: To assist the Host and have on-the-job training with the intent to be a Host.

Possibilities:
• Share weekly leadership within the group with the Host (selected questions, opening discussion, closing prayer time, etc.).
• Regularly rotate the leadership of the group (once or twice a month).
• Eventually start a new short-term group.

Profile: Shepherd's heart, servant leadership, spiritual walk, and spirit of humility.

Ministry Role

Purpose: To champion the individual SHAPE discovery process inside the group and around the church.

1 Corinthians 12:7; Ephesians 4:11–13; 1 Peter 3:10

Primary Function: To encourage everyone in the group to discover their ministry (through SHAPE) and coordinate periodic group service opportunities (at the church or to other believers).

Possibilities:
• Place each member into a group role or "baby step" responsibility.
• Challenge members to attend CLASS 301 and to complete the SHAPE interview process.
• Celebrate discovery, development, and deployment of next steps.
• Do ministry projects.

Profile: Cheerleader, goal-oriented, *and* loves to see people develop and grow themselves.

Fellowship Role

Purpose: To champion the fellowship and community-building activities within the small group.

Ephesians 2:19; Hebrews 10:24–25

Primary Function: To encourage the group to discover community and transparency by welcoming newcomers, honoring people, and deepening personal sharing.

Possibilities:
• Coordinate group socials and celebrations (birthdays, dinners, and group activities).
• Follow up on new and absent people with calls and cards.
• Manage the group roster and Small Group Guidelines and Agreement.

Profile: Social, fun-loving, encouraging, and has hospitality gifts.

Evangelism Role

Purpose: To champion outreach to the unconnected/unchurched in your community and around the world.

Matthew 28:18–20; Acts 20:24

Primary Function: To encourage the sharing of Christ through the PEACE Plan (personal, local, and global).

Possibilities:
• Encourage members to pray for unchurched friends or family members.
• Encourage members to invite an unchurched friend or neighbor to your group (to fill the open chair).
• Make the small group aware of mission prayer requests and/or participate in short-term mission projects.
• Adopt the PEACE Plan in your group.

Profile: Includer and bringer, heart for people (especially unconnected/unchurched people in our country and around the world) and cross-cultural experiences and involvement.

Discipleship Role

Purpose: To champion the spiritual growth and personal next steps of each member in your group.

Ephesians 4:15; Colossians 1:28

Primary Function: To encourage the overall spiritual formation process of your group by encouraging various spiritual exercises, experiences, or practices that will enhance each member's spiritual growth.

Possibilities:
• Encourage people to take their next step in CLASS (101, 201, 301, 401, 501).
• Encourage people to complete the Spiritual Health Assessment and Growth Plan.
• Share progress and plans about individual time with God and his Word (spiritual habits).
• Have spiritual partners.

Profile: Loves learning, heart for the Word, and desires a growing walk with God.

Worship Role

Purpose: To champion the purpose of worship and whole-life surrender in your small group.

John 4:24; Romans 12:1–2

Primary Function: To encourage the group to experience worship in a wide variety of ways; understanding that worship is more than music.

Possibilities:
• Coordinate a weekly praise and prayer list.
• Encourage members to personally cultivate their individual worship time with God (praise and worship CDs/DVDs in their home or car).
• Coordinate your group attending worship services together in community. (Encourage people to attend in subgroups of two to four, if not all together.)
• Host a communion service or worship time for your small group (CD, instruments, or a cappella).

Profile: Encourager, heart for personal and corporate worship, desires a deeper walk with God through prayer, and enjoys music and singing.

whether people are acting on the vision you have cast. But don't bog down the process with reporting. Rather, train all of your group members to inspect each other in love, spurring each other on toward greater love and good deeds (see Heb. 10:24–25). And you can help individuals become self-inspectors by putting tools in their hands like Saddleback's Spiritual Health Assessment and Spiritual Health Planner.

Develop Members into Leaders

Please see pages 86–89, "Instructions for Question Planning Pages," for how to fill this out.

Suggested Tasks	**CRAWL**	**Round out the leader:** *Pray for one future leader ("coleader," "apprentice," or untitled) from each small group, and ask each small group leader to identify and develop such a person.*
	WALK	**Roles for everyone:** *Set a goal for every group to informally give ownership of the five biblical purposes to different members.*
	RUN	**Rotate leadership:** *Encourage leaders to give other members the opportunity to lead a small portion of the meeting or sometimes entire meetings.*

Your Dream	Obstacles	Actions	Timing
Long-Range (1–5 years)			
Short-Range (1–12 months)			
	Other Actions		

After you've completed this page, mark the highest-priority action for this planning question. Copy that action onto the prioritizing list, pages 221–23 in chapter 10.

Q10 How Will Subgrouping Develop People?

We invest in people, in part, by developing their relationship with God and developing the gifting God has given them. This helps them clarify their purpose and help others. Some of this happens best when individuals and their gifts are "discovered," and these discoveries are more likely to happen among smaller numbers of people, such as when you use subgrouping (see figure 7.3).

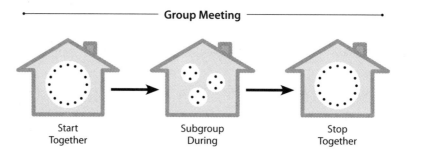

Group Meeting

Figure 7.3

Start Together   Subgroup During   Stop Together

Subgrouping is using part of the meeting time to divide into smaller, separate groups for any purpose. The whole group typically starts and ends together but breaks into subgroups somewhere in the middle. The purpose for subgrouping is to create situations with few enough people that each individual gets a chance to talk and quieter people are more willing to talk. A fundamental rule we give new Hosts is that if not everyone in your group has a chance to talk, then it's time to subgroup. Generally, this happens when groups grow to seven or more people.

Men's and Women's Subgroups

Subgroups can be formed any way you want. At Saddleback Church we've discovered special advantages in having men and women meet separately for part of some small group meetings. Besides the advantages of smaller numbers, women tend to share more openly with other women, and men with other men.

Saddleback used to have distinct men's and women's ministries, but we have done away with them. We still absolutely value the spiritual development of men and women, but we've found that when we call something a "ministry," it becomes just one more event for people to attend during their limited time. In addition, different ministries can become separate fiefdoms.

We have found that the best men's and women's connections develop in mixed-gender small groups of couples and singles, especially when subgrouping is used to give men some time with men and women with women.

My friend Jason Williams shared this story:

In our group's third meeting, right up front, we wanted to emphasize praying for each other. But the other wives told Joy (my wife) that their husbands would *never* pray out loud, or even talk, in the group. We decided on subgrouping, meeting separately as men and women for prayer time. Guys often feel safer around other guys, and we hoped this might create a space in which they'd give it a go. After we split and the men shared a few prayer requests, I told them I would love for us guys to be committed to praying for each other and wanted to set that tone right now. I explained that there is no right or wrong way to pray, that prayer is simply a conversation with our Father, who loves spending time with us. Just a sentence or two would more than suffice. Then I held my breath . . . and prayed God would prompt just one of them to break the ice.

After a minute that felt like an hour, one guy said, "God, I want to make a prayer for my friend Eric." Don't you just love hearing an honest prayer by someone who hasn't learned the polished "right way"? I was so thankful, and ready to jump in and close. But before I could, another guy chimed in. Then another. And another. I was stunned. By the time I closed, every guy had overcome his fear, taken a risk, and prayed. Subgrouping created a smaller, safer place. I will never forget that meeting.

In my own small group, one evening the men and women met separately for prayer. One woman admitted she was attracted to someone other than her husband. The women prayed over her and agreed to continued prayer and accountability. Later that night Lisa shared the woman's experience with me privately. Eventually the group came around the couple and helped save their marriage, which is now stronger than ever.

I believe this happened both because we, as couples, had developed intimacy that some women's groups don't have, but also because we gave the women the chance to be alone together. Subgrouping within the larger group was the key to investing in these people's lives.

Ideas for Subgrouping

You don't have to use subgroups every meeting—only as often as it is helpful for your group, sometimes just to add variety and avoid stagnation. And you can vary the timing and purpose. Anything is possible, but I see three great opportunities for subgrouping to take your group deeper:

1. *Fellowship.* Any activities a group does to build relationships and encourage each other can be done in subgroups—anything from snack and chat time to a ladies' or men's night out.
2. *Discussion.* Whatever type of curriculum or study style you use, part or all of the discussion time can be in subgroups. After Saddleback groups watch the evening's video together, they may break up to discuss the accompanying questions. Some topics lend themselves to discussion in subgroups of the same gender, stage of life, profession, or other characteristics.
3. *Prayer.* As we've seen, sharing and prayer often feel safer among fewer people, especially those we trust or who share some affinity.

Q10 Planning Page

Subgrouping to Develop People

Please see pages 86–89, "Instructions for Question Planning Pages," for how to fill this out.

Suggested Tasks		
CRAWL	**Groups:** *Encourage all groups of four or more to use subgrouping for some of their prayer times.*
WALK	**Planning:** *Plan small group meetings so there are regular opportunities to subgroup by gender.*
RUN	**Implementation:** *Assuming the cooperation of church leadership, transition your men's and women's ministries into gender-based large group/small group formats.*

Your Dream	Obstacles	Actions	Timing
Long-Range (1–5 years)			
Short-Range (1–12 months)			
	Other Actions		

After you've completed this page, mark the highest-priority action for this planning question. Copy that action onto the prioritizing list, pages 221–23 in chapter 10.

Q11 How Will You Encourage People to Serve?

People often fail to serve, not because they don't want to serve but because they feel they have nothing to offer or they have not been offered specific opportunities. Churches are full of overworked pastors and underused members. That is not God's plan, and it has been a problem as far back as Exodus 18, when Jethro taught Moses to delegate. Jesus clearly wants us to serve. He commands us to love our neighbors as ourselves (see Matt. 22:39). And when the church was birthed, "All the believers . . . had everything in common. They sold property and possessions to give to anyone who had need" (Acts 2:44–45). Service was normative in the early church.

I love Paul's teaching that all of the saints are meant to be prepared by leadership "for works of service" and that the body of Christ achieves unity and maturity, "attaining to the whole measure of the fullness of Christ" as "the whole body . . . grows and builds itself up in love, *as* each part does its work" (Eph. 4:12–13, 16, emphasis added). And Peter taught, "Each of you should use whatever gift you have received to serve others, as faithful stewards of God's grace in its various forms" (1 Pet. 4:10).

One universal human need is for *significance*—to have a purpose, to make a difference. So the case for service is based not only on the needs of the receivers, but also on the giver's needs. People have a need to exercise their gifts, to attain a sense of meaning in making a difference. And, of course, they also meet others' needs.

Every human is wired with a personality and special set of natural talents, and through life they are shaped further by their experiences. Then at salvation every follower of Christ also receives spiritual gifts. But people need a path to discovering their unique design and how best to use it for God's kingdom. Many people in your small groups are probably unaware of the ways God has prepared them for service (see Eph. 2:10). At Saddleback we offer CLASS 301 to help people discover their SHAPE—their *Spiritual gifts, Heart (passions), Abilities, Personality,* and *Experiences*—their unique design and function in the church body.

If your church doesn't have a way to help members uncover this, I encourage you to develop a method or find one and use it. People can work through this discovery process in small groups or outside, in a class or other venue. Everyone is a "ten" at something, and people find new fulfillment and make eternal impact when they begin serving in ways for which they were tailor-made.

Everyone is a "ten" at something.

At Saddleback we also introduced "Test-Drive a Ministry." We post service opportunities and encourage people to test-drive one for six weeks, putting their toe in the water and discovering what they like. We don't hold them to the full six weeks if they seriously dislike it.

Grow Servants in Your Small Groups

The healthiest and most effective small groups don't limit their identity to two hours per week. They live out their group identity 24/7. The 24/7 group doesn't just meet, study, and eat cookies—they live life together and take life deeper outside the meeting. Together they help each other fulfill Jesus's Great Commission and great commandment all week long.

I was so blessed by this letter from Glen Telusma of Freeport Bible Church in the Bahamas:

> I'm coaching three small groups that have done many "acts of kindness" in our community, such as giving people tokens to wash clothes, handing out bags of peanuts, and working with the elderly. The response has been incredible. Not only have we been able to take care of those in our small group ministry, but our community as well. I have also been the recipient of kindness. I had major surgery, and my group rallied up in support. Our church has come a mighty long way.

The fact is, you have a *ton* of hidden talent sitting in your small group ministry. It is your job, and the job of your leaders, to uncover those talents and help group members develop them in a God-glorifying, kingdom-building way.

Sometimes surprising talent is right under your nose. Way back when we were starting our first satellite campus in San Clemente, we had no idea how to handle the technological aspects of multisite ministry. Through a strange series of God-ordained "coincidences," we discovered that the very person we needed—the owner of a recommended tech company—lived in our city and was, in fact, a Saddleback member who was involved and serving in a small group! He brought his talent to meet our need for broadcasting to our multisite campuses.

Don't wait for resources to come to you. For the sake of all members and your church, make it a priority to unlock and then utilize them. God gave these resources to your church for a reason, and we do not want to squander a single opportunity to glorify him.

Train your leaders to nurture servanthood in their groups and service opportunities within the church and your ministry. Use every opportunity with leaders to encourage and help them challenge their group members to sacrifice beyond themselves.

Campaigns are another way to focus your church beyond themselves, helping others, if you have (or can win) the cooperation of your senior leadership. We hardwire into every campaign's small group curriculum a service opportunity for every group. We've found that when small groups serve together, their rate for staying together goes from 68 to 83 percent. Serving together helps others, but it's also good for the group.

Q11 Planning Page

Encourage People to Serve

Please see pages 86–89, "Instructions for Question Planning Pages," for how to fill this out.

Suggested Tasks		
CRAWL	**Individuals:** *Use a study or tool, like SHAPE, in all small groups to help every member discover how God has uniquely designed them for service.*
WALK	**Groups:** *Challenge each group to own the basic needs of its members (for example, babysitting for needy moms, transporting the elderly to appointments).*
RUN	**Ministry:** *Develop a ministrywide pattern of celebrating servant-hood—simple but meaningful ways of publicly honoring (and fueling) servants.*

Your Dream	Obstacles	Actions	Timing
Long-Range (1–5 years)			
Short-Range (1–12 months)			
	Other Actions		

After you've completed this page, mark the highest-priority action for this planning question. Copy that action onto the prioritizing list, pages 221–23 in chapter 10.

 **How Will You Create Opportunities for Groups to Serve?**

Serving together strengthens camaraderie, *esprit de corps*, and bonds among group members. Working together toward a common goal—especially venturing outside comfort zones—creates relationship-deepening memories, strengthens the group's sense of unity and identity, and fosters trust, especially when service requires "having each other's backs." Serving together also makes members accountable for follow-through. With the right motivation, no one wants to be left out.

Spontaneous Opportunities

If you succeed in fostering servant hearts throughout your small group ministry, members will be on the lookout for service opportunities that arise spontaneously. As an example, when my wife's dad had a major stroke, our group stepped in to care for our son while we were gone to care for Dad. Various people brought Ethan meals and took him to a movie. What a blessing!

Some group members have needs they're too prideful or embarrassed to share. You and your leaders can urge people to be willing to ask for help, giving others the blessing of helping.

But don't just expect your groups to find spontaneous opportunities on their own. I encourage you to be intentional in creating additional connections between your small groups and a wider variety of service opportunities.

Seasonal Opportunities

Seasonal opportunities can set groups up for a psychological win. Since the commitment is limited-time, people can sustain enthusiasm from beginning to end and celebrate quickly upon completion. Inform your groups about ways they can serve in your church or community at key, recurring times throughout the calendar year. You may choose certain events to give special attention and "swamp" with help, making sure there are plenty of hands on deck to meet the need in a loving and effective way.

For example, a small group may adopt a school classroom for a month to help with midterm needs. Contact a school or senior center to discover spring cleaning opportunities. In the fall provide backpacks filled with supplies for needy students in your church. Invite people without a family to Thanksgiving dinner. Adopt a needy family and provide a tree, decorations, and Christmas dinner.

Short-Term Opportunities

Some groups reach a point of readiness for a run-level service activity. At Saddleback our PEACE Plan draws many entire groups to do global and local short-term outreach as a group. The whole group doesn't have to go abroad in order to be involved. We encourage as many as possible to join the "away team"—the people who go. The rest of the group forms the "home team," supporting the away team in several vital ways. This prevents anyone from feeling guilty or left out because everyone contributes substantially. (For more on this, see "Home and Away Teams," pages 187–88.)

If you want a good return on investment, your small groups must start investing in people. Some of your groups (the early adopters) will catch on immediately with little prodding. To help the mid- and late adopters come on board, enlist your small group leaders and leader coaches to keep encouraging these groups to become strong links in your ministry chain.

Q12 Planning Page

Please see pages 86–89, "Instructions for Question Planning Pages," for how to fill this out.

Opportunities for Groups to Serve

Suggested Tasks		
CRAWL	**Spontaneous opportunities:** *Challenge each small group to find and fulfill a service opportunity in or outside the group.*	
WALK	**Seasonal opportunities:** *Challenge small groups to serve at Easter, Christmas, or church events.*	
RUN	**Short-term opportunities:** *Present small groups with short-term service opportunities (perhaps even projects at the church) for which they develop a "home and away" strategy.*	

Your Dream	Obstacles	Actions	Timing
Long-Range (1–5 years)			
Short-Range (1–12 months)			
	Other Actions		

After you've completed this page, mark the highest-priority action for this planning question. Copy that action onto the prioritizing list, pages 221–23 in chapter 10.

8

The Front Door

REACHING OTHERS THROUGH SMALL GROUPS

Q13—How Will You Promote Reach and Spiritual Awareness?

Q14—How Will You Engage Every Group in Global Outreach?

Q15—How Will You Engage Every Group in Local Outreach?

Q16—How Will You Involve Every Group in Personal Evangelism?

 How Will You Promote Reach and Spiritual Awareness?

The symbolism of a home's front door or entryway is powerful. This is the passage by which you bring people from outside into your home. "Outside" represents exposure to the elements and lack of safety and security. The church's evangelism is like your home's front door—the entryway for outside people to join in the health and security of the temple courts and house-to-house environments. In this part of your small group ministry plan, we talk about how you see those on the outside and start their journey inside.

I know this is a challenge because of what I've learned through my experience and from tens of thousands who rate themselves using Saddleback's Spiritual Health Assessment. I've discovered that in our fulfillment of Jesus's Great Commission and great commandment (in fellowship, discipleship, worship, ministry, and evangelism), people self-report that the most deficient area in their lives is evangelism.

If evangelism is one of the purposes of your small groups, this chapter (Q13–Q16) will give you principles and ideas for accomplishing that purpose. At Saddleback we seek to get every small group in mission outreach, engaging those outside the church, giving them a glimpse of what's inside. (They may not be like us, yet light attracts them.) However, many believers resist doing evangelism, largely because churches have missed what evangelism is. It's important to understand which role belongs to which person in evangelism—our role and God's role. Somehow we have forgotten what Paul wrote: "I planted the seed, Apollos watered it, but God has been making it grow. So neither the one who plants nor the one who waters is anything, but only God, who makes things grow" (1 Cor. 3:6–7). We can't change people—only God can. But he has called us to share his message and to love people in ways that plant and water seeds, giving more people the opportunity to accept him.

Most classes and sermons about evangelism are about closing the deal, making sure people come to faith in Jesus. Obviously this is the goal, but we forget that such a major life decision sometimes takes lots of preliminary

It's important to understand which role belongs to which person in evangelism— our role and God's role.

groundwork to lead the nonbeliever to readiness. If we aren't out there with nonbelievers, planting and watering, how can we expect to see God produce a harvest? Although the planter of the seed may never see the fruit of his or her labor, the ground has been prepared. It's the Holy Spirit's job to win people over.

So in spurring small groups toward outreach, we will focus predominantly on how to mobilize groups to plant and water—to love nonbelievers through all the weeks and years it often takes to build trust and overcome their misconceptions about Christianity. Whether it's an individual, a community, or even a nation, we can't win them to Christ until they believe we're their friend. Success in personal, local, and global outreach depends on building relationships through which God's love and truth can flow. You don't win your enemies to Christ, you win your friends.

So, though it's important to get God's people to church, let's not keep them so busy *doing* church that they aren't *being* the church to the world. Jesus made clear in his Great Commission what he expects from us: *Go!* We will examine ways that small groups can go globally, go locally, and go personally. Let's applaud them, wherever they go.

At Fuller Seminary I had the privilege of learning from C. Peter Wagner, a theologian, missionary, missiologist, and amazing man of God. His family was in agriculture, and one of the things he always taught was "farm to the fence line"—that is, maximize all the people, resources, and opportunities we are given.

Help your people see that every person they encounter is a God-given appointment. Some we see periodically (the dry cleaner, store cashier, manicurist), and some frequently (neighbors, sports enthusiasts, coworkers). Some are friends and family, part of our inner circles. They are at different places along their spiritual journey, and understanding each one's spiritual state is important in reaching them. Teach your people to recognize every outreach opportunity God puts in their lives. Sometimes we create these intentionally with people we know. And the Holy Spirit also uses spontaneous opportunities, even with people we don't know.

You don't win your enemies to Christ, you win your friends.

"Farming to the fence line" also means maximizing our talents. Encourage group members to list their talents and prayerfully look for ways to use them to reach nonbelievers. People who need Christ are more likely to open up to us if we open ourselves vulnerably to them. Sharing ourselves appropriately—the ways God has been important in our positive and negative experiences—will increase trust from people with like experiences.

Every Christian has 168 hours per week, part of it for doing "church stuff." We offer many programs and opportunities at church among other believers, and that's awesome. But this isn't "farming to the fence line." The nonbelievers we're supposed to be reaching aren't spending their time at church, so if Christians spend all their available time at church, how are we going to build relationships with non-Christians? Where are you spending your most precious resource—your people?

The world can be the mission field for your small group ministry—from your front doors to the farthest reaches. You can help your church define its global, local, and personal opportunities to evangelize, and then equip your groups to meet those needs.

Small Group Members Need to Know Their Circles

The circles in which we move through life are shown in figure 8.1. Some involve more time, some less. Some are voluntary, others obligatory. These are our spheres of influence among nonbelievers, our fields of evangelism. Train your leaders to make time in their groups to focus on thinking about the people in each of their circles. Ask them to write down and prayerfully reach out to:

- Family—near or far
- Friends
- Factory/firm—work associates
- Fun—people we meet through the gym, hobbies, sports leagues (ours or our kids')

Figure 8.1

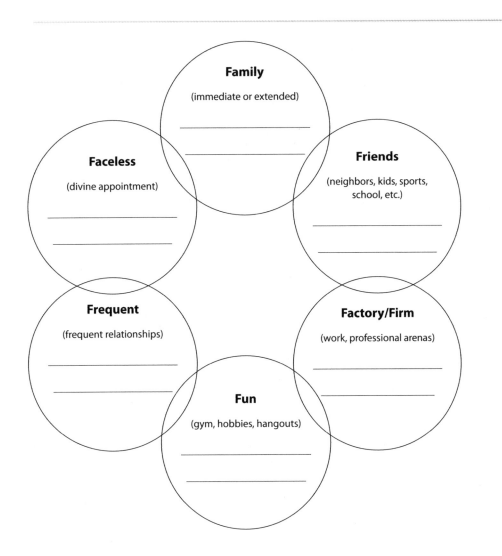

- Frequent—people we see frequently while running errands
- Faceless—anyone God brings across our path

I want you to hear from Tim Chambers, associate pastor at South End Fellowship Baptist Church in Owen Sound, Ontario, Canada. One of his circles (the Faceless) became real because he didn't ignore a name God brought into his circle:

In the fall of 2016 I sat with a group of men (as we did every week) in a local Tim Hortons coffee shop, and we prayed for the opportunity to lead people to Jesus. We prayed that the Spirit would make us sensitive to gospel opportunities.

On January 10, 2017, as I was driving to work on a frigidly cold morning, I noticed a guy walking along the road with a big bag in his arms. I kept driving. A bit further down the road I felt the Spirit urging me to turn around. I parked the car and prayed. I drove back to the stranger, introduced myself, and invited him (Seth) to hop in. He accepted and we had a great chat in the five-minute ride to his house. Along the way I mentioned that we had a men's breakfast coming up at church the following week.

Amazingly, Seth showed up to the breakfast! At the end of the morning I offered a new Bible to anyone who'd like one. Seth asked if he could have one and promised to start reading it that day.

Two weeks later, Seth and I went out to coffee to discuss what he had read. He told me he had finished reading Genesis and Exodus . . . and that he had no idea what he had read. I told Seth that if he was willing, I'd spend time helping him understand. The following Monday we met at the same coffee shop to read the first chapter of a book called *The Stranger on the Road to Emmaus*, which helps explain the big story of the Bible from creation to the cross.

Seth took his book home and laid it down on the coffee table, where his mother found it, and she read the first chapter for herself. Once finished, she asked Seth if she could come with him for the next study.

Two days later I met with both Seth and Sandra and we continued our study. For the next two months, we met every Monday, Wednesday, and Friday at 10 a.m. It was absolutely incredible watching the lightbulbs of understanding go on for both of them as the Spirit worked in their hearts.

The day we finished the book, they both trusted Jesus Christ as their Savior.

Our studies didn't stop there. We continued to meet three times a week to unpack what being a disciple of Jesus looks like.

But there were still hurdles along the way. Seth and Sandra both struggled with extreme social anxiety. When I invited them to church, they didn't come. They arrived at the church parking lot, saw how full it was, and bolted for home. The second week, no show. After the third no-show I decided that baby steps might be best.

I invited them in for a private tour of the church. They looked in every room, every office, every closet. We picked out seats at the back for them to sit in the next Sunday morning and created reserved seating signs. We picked out a parking spot that I blocked off specifically for them. The plan was for them to show up to the service late and leave during the closing prayer to help avoid the crowds.

The first service they showed up for was Easter Sunday. Over the weeks we've been able to drop all the special measures, and Seth and Sandra are coming to church faithfully without any hesitations. At the moment, we are preparing for their baptisms while watching them grow in leaps and bounds.

But the story doesn't end there.

Soon after Seth and Sandra began attending church, they invited a family friend with them. They started the same process of going through *The Stranger on the Road to Emmaus* with her. Just last week, as the four of us sat around my kitchen table, their friend made the decision to trust Jesus as her Savior.

This is more than I prayed for. I didn't know these people from Adam six months ago. Now they are family, here on earth and for eternity!!

Praise the Lord that he cares for the faceless people in our lives.

Keep in mind our crawl-walk-run philosophy, because some opportunities will be easier than others, and some circles are easier or harder for different people.

Q13 Planning Page

Promote Reach and Spiritual Awareness

Please see pages 86–89, "Instructions for Question Planning Pages," for how to fill this out.

Suggested Tasks		
	CRAWL	**Identify:** *Challenge leaders to have their group members fill out their circles of influence and identify one person to pray for.*
	WALK	**Touch:** *Challenge leaders to have their group members each choose one next step for bringing an unbeliever closer to seeing and knowing Christ.*
	RUN	**Share:** *Encourage small group members to share their stories of their outreach efforts with others. (Collect these from leaders for use throughout your ministry.)*

Your Dream	Obstacles	Actions	Timing
Long-Range (1–5 years)			
Short-Range (1–12 months)			
	Other Actions		

After you've completed this page, mark the highest-priority action for this planning question. Copy that action onto the prioritizing list, pages 221–23 in chapter 10.

How Will You Engage Every Group in Global Outreach?

At Saddleback we use the PEACE Plan for global outreach.

Global Giants and Their Antidotes

Figure 8.2

	Plant churches that promote reconciliation	**E**quip servant leaders	**A**ssist the poor	**C**are for the sick	**E**ducate the next generation
Local Church Initiated	*to address the giant of* **spiritual emptiness**	*to address the giant of* **self-serving leadership**	*to address the giant of* **poverty**	*to address the giant of* **disease**	*to address the giant of* **illiteracy**

PEACE—doing all the things Jesus did

The Spirit of the Lord is on me [Jesus], because he has anointed me to proclaim good news to the poor. He has sent me to proclaim freedom for the prisoners and recovery of sight for the blind, to set the oppressed free, to proclaim the year of the Lord's favor.
Luke 4:18–19 (NIV)

Figure 8.2 shows how Saddleback is attacking the five global giants of spiritual emptiness, self-serving leaders, poverty, disease, and illiteracy. We send groups out to other countries and partner with national churches—making the national church the hero, not us. We understand that not everyone feels ready for a foreign mission field, but everyone can help those who travel.

Home and Away Teams

Any global or local group outreach project is a sizeable effort. I recommend a two-team strategy that makes the undertaking easier and more inviting to groups. This helps increase whole-group buy-in because everyone feels a part of the mission.

Not everyone in the group can go on trips because of kids, work schedules, or other life demands. But people want to participate and make a difference. So while a group's *away team* gets ready and goes on the trip, the *home team* may:

- Pray for the away team
- Fast a meal for the away team
- Help the away team prepare
- Feed the away team's pets, take the kids on errands, get mail, and so on
- Check on the away team's homes, if needed

This strategy makes everyone a real part of the trip. Even if only a few travel, they are backed by their whole group.

Through the global PEACE Plan we adopt a country, become a friend to the nationals, and concentrate our efforts to attack the global giants. This isn't one trip and done but rather a strategy accomplished through ongoing relationships with the national church. We attack the giants by planting churches, promoting reconciliation, equipping servant leaders (destroying corruption), assisting the poor through microenterprise, caring for the sick, and educating the next generation holistically. Learn more about the PEACE Plan at www.ThePeacePlan.com.

Your church may already use a different approach. My point here is to challenge small groups to mobilize for global outreach—a win for everyone.

Other Global Opportunities

Besides sending teams overseas, small groups can also:

- Choose a missionary, a country, or an unreached or unengaged people group to pray for
- Have members research and report on the target country, people group, or other global cause

- Prepare a meal or taste of culture from the target country
- Visit a restaurant representing the target people group
- Sponsor a needy person, school, or other institution in the target country
- Communicate with a missionary by mail, email, social media, video calls, and the like
- Support Bible translation for the target people group
- Have fun learning the target group's or country's language. Group members can do this by learning short phrases, sharing an interesting fact about the people group or country, or learning the foreign letters that spell their names.

These help groups think globally without boarding a plane.

Q14 Planning Page

Engage Groups in Global Outreach

Please see pages 86–89, "Instructions for Question Planning Pages," for how to fill this out.

Suggested Tasks		
CRAWL	**Learn**: *Challenge all groups to research and learn about a country or unreached people group.*
WALK	**Pray**: *Challenge all groups to pray regularly for a country or unreached people group.*
RUN	**Go**: *Challenge all groups to prayerfully consider implementing a "home and away team" strategy for a global mission trip.*

Your Dream	Obstacles	Actions	Timing
Long-Range (1–5 years)			
Short-Range (1–12 months)			
	Other Actions		

After you've completed this page, mark the highest-priority action for this planning question. Copy that action onto the prioritizing list, pages 221–23 in chapter 10.

How Will You Engage Every Group in Local Outreach?

Local outreach is a bit easier because generally the time commitment is lower and travel means a drive rather than a flight. We are all keenly aware of the needs in our communities, towns, cities, and region, so it just takes a bit of research and some coordination for a small group to make a big impact.

Local Outreach Opportunities

These service opportunities are available throughout your community and region, and some appeal to passions among small group members.

Community Needs

Help your community see your church as a friend. Get to know your city officials, ask them about needs your small groups can address, and then mobilize your people.

School Needs

There is not a school on this planet that couldn't use some help. Imagine if each of your small groups adopted a classroom, perhaps in a small way (providing supplies) or a big way (tutoring, coaching). Consider starting with the school attended by kids or grandkids of group members.

Events

Every town, city, or community coordinates a variety of events with which your small groups could help. The city of Lake Forest put on "I Love Lake Forest," so our Lake Forest campus joined in—helping in many ways, from letting them use our parking to helping with promotion. Guess what? They gave us an event booth for free.

Holidays

You can be light in a dark world during any holiday, even building friendships with people of other faiths—bridges across which Jesus can walk. Your group can adopt families at Christmas, minister to needs at Thanksgiving, and provide practical assistance for families and organizations at other special times.

Passion Areas

My friend Kevin loves to play basketball. He offers a free clinic to teach disadvantaged kids fundamental skills of the sport. He takes his clinic to a Native American reservation, and through his years developing this relationship, he has created inroads for our twelve-step ministry, Celebrate Recovery, on the reservation. He turned his passion into a local opportunity to bring PEACE. Your people can too!

Crises

Small groups can be the hands and feet of the church to offer peace.

Many of today's crises come in two categories—environmental and sociological. Your small groups can mobilize to help in either type by such activities as collecting supplies and transporting people. The "home and away" team strategy is sometimes helpful. Unfortunately, crises never tell us they are coming, so you have to be ready. Each region faces some type of natural disaster, such as earthquakes and fires in Southern California, so our church remains prepared to call on our small groups in such events. Some regions are prone to racial conflict, sometimes needing local churches to pray and offer assistance. Small groups can be the hands and feet of the church to offer peace. Heaven is going to be filled with every race, so let's practice here on earth.

One-Day Trips

My friend Kurt Johnson explains the power of a local, short-term trip:

God has been tugging on my heart for a few years regarding a short-term mission trip to serve the less fortunate. I've listened to our pastor, Rick Warren, preach that we are "blessed to be a blessing," and that we always receive more blessing in return. I knew that serving together would strengthen relationships within my family and coworkers. I started a community service program at my company and volunteered my family for local service projects, like the Saddleback Food Pantry.

But God's voice was getting louder, asking me to commit to a short-term mission trip. Recently I heard about one-day mission trips to Mexico. I introduced the idea to our weekly workplace Bible study, and through them to all other employees. We gathered a team of thirteen, ranging in age from ten to fifty-four.

We met at 4:45 a.m. on a Saturday and drove two and a half hours in vans to La Mision, Baja California, Mexico. During the morning we did light construction work on a new medical center. At lunch we went down the road and served over a hundred children an American-style hamburger meal. I've never seen anyone so excited about a Costco burger. Then we hung out and played with the kids, on their terms. After lots of hugs and heartfelt goodbyes, we headed back north to our lives of luxury and convenience. My best memories were the people I care about serving and pouring love into the kids. And a stoic three-year-old named Hector saying "more" every time I stopped pushing his swing. These kids can soften even the hardest hearts.

We came back with fresh perspective and a renewed appreciation for God's everyday blessings. I wanted to help the less fortunate, but I also wanted my family and coworkers to experience the joy of serving, knowing that they would benefit. And, truth be told, I wanted my teenagers to understand how good they have it here in the land of bling. It was a success on all counts.

I learned that God made us to serve, not just because the world needs it, but because we need it. Whenever we live out our design, we connect on a deep level with God and people. *And serving others brings healing.* All of us can serve others, no matter our station in life. This fit nicely with my understanding that serving others is partly a self-serving pursuit. Jesus's parable of the talents (Matt. 25:14–30 ESV) teaches that investment in God's kingdom will be rewarded many times over. That's pretty self-serving. But God made us that way, and he doesn't make mistakes.

Q15 Planning Page

Engage Groups in Local Outreach

Please see pages 86–89, "Instructions for Question Planning Pages," for how to fill this out.

Suggested Tasks		
CRAWL	**Schools:** *Have each group identify a school that they can contact to help in a small way for a semester (maybe adopting one classroom).*	
WALK	**Communities:** *Have your groups contact their community officials to do a one-time project to serve and build relationships.*	
RUN	**Trips:** *Challenge groups to do a half-day or one-day local mission trip using the "home and away" strategy to engage every group member.*	

Your Dream	Obstacles	Actions	Timing
Long-Range (1–5 years)			
Short-Range (1–12 months)			
	Other Actions		

After you've completed this page, mark the highest-priority action for this planning question. Copy that action onto the prioritizing list, pages 221–23 in chapter 10.

How Will You Involve Every Group in Personal Evangelism?

We should all be sharing our faith, and this personal evangelism is an important prerequisite to "bigger" outreach efforts. I like to say, "People need to learn to cross the street before they cross the sea." God calls each of his people to build loving relationships with his or her community and circles of influence—clubs, workplaces, and anywhere else we spend time with people.

Here are a few ways small groups can grow in personal evangelism:

- Ask each member to identify a person they know who doesn't know Christ, and then challenge them to deepen that relationship, hopefully planting seeds of truth and watering them for the Lord's ultimate harvest.

- Have the group members map their neighborhoods, listing the names in each home and their possible spiritual status. The website www .Pray4EveryHome.com can help track who lives in their area.

- Map each member's work environment or people with whom he or she engages in a typical week.

- Plan a small group party and invite a few people who don't know Christ so they can see Christians having fun without being "religious."

- Take the group to a sporting event, or watch one on TV, and invite nonbelievers to join you.

- Throw a community block party, inviting small group members even if they don't live on the block.

- Study Mark 2:15–17 to inspire ideas for a reach event.

All small group members should have a strategy for spending time with and befriending those who need Christ. All of Scripture calls us to love our neighbors. Great commandment, anyone?

People need to learn to cross the street before they cross the sea.

195

Speak

When I say "evangelism," don't picture standing outside your house with a John 3:16 sign. Don't overcomplicate the *how*; focus on *who*. Encourage groups to have members list names and pray for opportunities to have normal conversations with them, using the **SPEAK** pattern that Rick Warren teaches:

Story—Ask people to tell their story, because we all love to talk about ourselves. Let them start from wherever they want, because that way they will be more comfortable.

Passions—Listen as they talk, and uncover their passions and what they like to do with their time. What in life excites them?

Encouragement—As you hear their stories and discover their passions, listen, with eye contact, for ways they may need to be encouraged.

Abilities—What talents do they have, maybe related to work, hobbies, sports, and other interests?

Knowledge—Everyone knows something you don't. You just need to ask the right questions. Ask about what they're watching or reading, their education, apps they use, and so on.

When you have a conversation, keep these five letters in mind. These steps will show you care and will open doors for you to share your story, God's story, and the power of Jesus in your life.

The Power of a Story

We have talked a lot about using stories throughout this book, and for a good reason! Story is a powerful medium to help drive a point home. Remember that Jesus used stories to communicate a point. Train your small group members to use their personal stories for evangelism. When they tell their story to nonbelievers, they show they believe the gospel themselves, and they demonstrate how Jesus has changed their lives.

Your story is just that—*your* story, whatever you've experienced, especially the love of God. After Jesus encountered the woman at the well (John 4) and after he healed the blind man (John 9), people simply told about what they experienced, their encounter with Jesus.

Now the best time to first tell your story is long before it counts with a nonbeliever! Have small groups practice ahead of time with each other. (Members will also learn more about each other.) Each member should write or somehow record his or her story as a way of thinking it through. A good outline is:

1. Before I knew Christ
2. How I met Christ
3. How Christ helps me now

Everyone should develop a quick, five- or ten-minute version and also a detailed version. We never know what time frame the Lord will give us.

Q16 Planning Page

Involve Groups in Personal Evangelism

Please see pages 86–89, "Instructions for Question Planning Pages," for how to fill this out.

Suggested Tasks		
CRAWL	**Develop stories:** *Challenge every group member to develop a five-minute version of his or her story, based on the three-part outline above. Have every member practice telling the story to the group, then pray for opportunities to share it with unbelievers.*
WALK	**Map communities:** *Challenge each group to map their community, as described above, and then to pray for each household as we would pray for our families.*
RUN	**Reach events:** *Give groups a list of ideas, and challenge each group to do a simple reach event, inviting nonbelievers just to have fun with believers.*

Your Dream	Obstacles	Actions	Timing
Long-Range (1–5 years)			
Short-Range (1–12 months)			
	Other Actions		

After you've completed this page, mark the highest-priority action for this planning question.
Copy that action onto the prioritizing list, pages 221–23 in chapter 10.

9

The Dining Room

SUSTAINING LONG-TERM SUCCESS IN SMALL GROUPS

Q17—How Will You Ensure Your Ministry's Long-Term Success?

Q18—How Will You Celebrate Stories of Life Change to Reach Your Vision?

Q19—How Will You Remain True to Your Call?

Q20—How Will You Help Your Groups Cultivate an Attitude of Worshipful Submission?

Now what? What do you do once your small group ministry is up and running? How do you sustain your ministry in a way that continually challenges you and your members? How, in the growth and retention cycles of church life, do you keep your vision and mission central? How do you make sure your compass is set and you stay on course through the storms?

Starting small groups is one task. Sustaining and building them for health is yet another, and in some ways trickier. You can't microwave a small group ministry. If God wants to grow a mushroom, he does it in six hours. If God wants to grow an oak tree, he does it in sixty years. If you want a small group ministry like a mushroom, soft and easily destroyed, grow it quickly. If you'd rather have a ministry like an oak tree—with deep roots, strength, and longevity—it will take more time. We've been refining our small group ministry for twenty years. Sometimes it feels like 120 years, and sometimes it feels like twenty minutes. It takes time to do it right! Pray for the people working with you. Pray that you will plan your goals with wise intentionality. And if your goals don't scare you, they aren't big enough. Pray for perseverance as you labor to accomplish those scary goals. Then let God move you!

For example, Chris McCall, small groups and care pastor at Watermark Church, Ashford, Alabama, explains in a recent note how his church added leader coaching and support as a way of sustaining long-term success:

> Our small groups ministry seemed to be OK, but something was missing. Our small groups had become stagnant, and we were losing almost the same number of groups we were starting. Our leaders were not getting the span of care they so desperately needed. We had tried a coaching structure on numerous occasions, but it typically died a quick, painful death because we had made it about the structure, not the people. After many discussions I knew we needed another go at coaching with a different tactic.
>
> I enlisted some great group leaders that were very relational and were on board with small groups. These became our small groups leadership team and our first generation of community leaders. Our crawl phase was to spend time vision casting, training, and building on our relationships. During the walk phase we placed the community leaders over group leaders with whom they already had relationships. Last, we launched the run phase by placing unfamiliar group leaders under their care. This has already created a great deal of momentum in our ministry. We are now adding more groups than we're losing, and next semester we will begin adding the second generation of community leaders.

This is the goal. A healthy, strong, growing small group ministry that is sustained through the changing experiences of life.

If your goals don't scare you, they aren't big enough.

How Will You Ensure Your Ministry's Long-Term Success?

Q17

Did you know that NASA schedules course corrections at various times during a rocket's flight? Modern space travel succeeds by periodically checking their trajectory and making any necessary adjustments to successfully reach the destination.

Much like NASA, we need to make small corrections along our journey. Some corrections help bring the ministry back on plan after it has drifted. This keeps you following your plotted course.

But sometimes you may realize that the plan itself needs to be revised because experience shows the original plan to be inadequate or that you've outgrown it. This is a natural part of ministry, because you can't know everything when you first launch out. A plan that needs to be changed is not a failure, and you don't need to feel guilty unless you fail to update a plan that isn't working. Every church is different, so developing your small group ministry is an expedition into uncharted waters. It's common to experience what feel like setbacks to our plans. "Setbacks" are often, in actuality, the unveiling of God's plans and the opening of doors we never knew existed. When this happens, take the new insight as a gift from God to bring you closer to the plan he had all along.

Your small group ministry will not course correct by itself. Ministry corrections are needed all the time. You can't take a bunch of imperfect people and create a perfect small group ministry or church. Sometimes the called-for adjustments seem impossible, and they are often frustrating. It's hard to stay the course. What will keep you motivated? Your vision and mission! Your dream and your purpose! Be willing to make constant course corrections in your plan and ultimately grow your ministry into what God means it to be.

Your small group ministry will not course correct by itself.

Define Success, Stay Aligned

Your church vision and mission define success for your church. Because of this, you need to keep your ministry aligned with your church, its temple courts, and all of its other ministries. If each part doesn't understand the roles the others play, or if one part is out of sync, everyone falls out of sync. Keep building relational capital with the rest of your church's leadership and other ministries. Do what you can to foster interconnected cooperation in which each part helps the others work together to maximize your church's kingdom achievement.

The vision and mission of your small group ministry will define that ministry's contribution to your church's success. This is your strong foundation on which you will build. If you ever toss the blueprints and freestyle it, you are going to end up with a mess. It's important to stay the course and work your plan, all the while allowing room for adjustments, both yours and God's. As your ministry grows, you will sometimes have to evaluate whether your blueprints permit the ministry equivalent of an extra living room or bigger kitchen. But overall, you must stay aligned with your original vision and mission.

Here are a few ways to detect needed adjustments or to confirm that you're on course:

- Schedule regular evaluations, especially with your C Team. Ask, "Are we on course, or do we need to adjust course to get back on plan?" And ask the harder question, "Do we need to revise the plan?" Keep applying a critical eye both to where you are and to where you want to go.

- Use surveys, questionnaires, and other data sources to measure intended outcomes. Too many can exhaust leaders, so we use no more than three or four surveys a year to monitor the effectiveness of tools we offer, group health, and overall satisfaction.

- Interview randomly selected small group members and leaders to get glimpses into the state of group life. You yourself should do some of this because it's appropriate for the shepherd (pastor) to mingle with the sheep.

- Consider conducting exit interviews or surveys of members who've left groups or leaders who've stepped out of leadership. Sometimes their reasons for leaving are unrelated to the ministry's effectiveness, but sometimes you'll receive helpful feedback for adjustments.

- Ask other ministries in the church how you are doing at partnering with them and together helping people become more like Christ.

You may not always know how to address problems that come to light. Consider gaining fresh outside perspective from new sources beyond your leadership team—trusted friends, leaders from other churches, other leaders in your church, and of course your senior pastor.

When you implement change, always do it with relationships in mind. You want to build relationships with the people the change is affecting. You are serving the Lord and people, not just accomplishing tasks. And always overcommunicate. People will be down on whatever they are not up on.

Guard against Drift

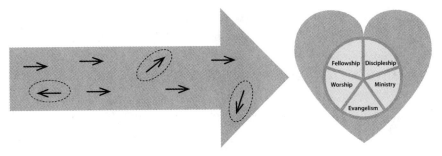

Figure 9.1

It's not uncommon for someone to become complacent after a long time in any ministry. The heart shown in figure 9.1 represents Saddleback's definition of the mature disciple, and it reminds us of our target when we lose perspective. Your church should keep in mind the kind of person you are hoping to produce (see Q5). The large arrow is the overall vision and mission of your church. The smaller arrows within the larger arrow are the direction your church's ministries are headed. Therefore, each ministry within your church should be nurturing people toward this goal. Unfortunately, you may find yourself in a place of conflict, where some ministries are a little off and others may actually be working against the intended end of developing complete disciples for your church. Do your best to work together toward unity and fresh clarity of purpose.

Any time you're leading others toward a goal, follow-up is key. It's a mistake to issue an instruction without checking back to make sure it was carried out.

Understand the Levels of Renewal

Renewal in your small group ministry starts with you! God has you at your church to build the house-to-house component talked about in the book of Acts. In order to enact the frequent "upgrades" required to keep your ministry on course, you need to understand and implement the five levels of renewal:

1. *Personal renewal.* For you, the point person for your small group ministry, this begins with confession. This is renewal of your vertical connection with God, which must happen before anything else. Your soul is cleansed, recharged, and open for God's marching orders. This is where God can build your passion and conviction to stoke your ministry's fire. You are the conscience of the small group ministry. You give it direction and momentum. If the enemy gets you off task, he has won. You should also ensure that personal renewal is reduplicated throughout your ministry leadership.

2. *Relational renewal.* The church economy deals in the currency of relationships, and relationships deepen as people spend time together and come to know each other better. As the ministry point person, you need to build your relational currency with all of your leadership. As a member of your church's leadership, you must build relational currency with other leaders and ministries. Do all you can to foster relational depth through all parts of your ministry, in every direction, among all participants.

3. *Missional renewal.* This is where you help all the people understand your purpose, why your small group ministry exists. You fire up

your veterans and ministry champions (early adopters), allow fence sitters (mid-adopters) space to understand, and give the resistant (late adopters) a vantage point to see the value of your ministry's purpose. Missional renewal is never finished; it's an ongoing process that varies in intensity.

4. *Structural renewal*. As your ministry grows, its original structure will not survive, because it shouldn't. A ministry of fifty small groups can't thrive in the same structure that served well for five groups. Be prepared to change the way you handle administration, communication, training, budgeting, and other aspects of programming.

5. *Cultural renewal*. Understand that drift always happens, and once-aligned ministries can become misaligned. There is a spiritual parallel with the second law of thermodynamics, which says that the total entropy of the universe is constantly increasing toward disorder, never decreasing toward order. People are people, and our fallen nature takes over. In cultural renewal, your mission and vision stoke the fire and bring all teams and departments back on course. All parts come to understand how they fit in the Acts 5:42 temple courts and house-to-house strategy, and all do their parts to champion each other.

Many pastors and ministry leaders make a common mistake. They may be working hard at the level of personal renewal, and maybe everyone under their leadership is doing the same. That's good. Then they attend a conference or read a book about how to do church or small group ministry, and they go straight to structural renewal, trying to change everything. They skip over the intervening levels of renewal. They may envision a wonderful structure, but since they've skipped over renewal of relationships, mission, and culture, no one else sees the reason or feels the motivation to adopt the new structure. The whole population must move along together through all five stages, and structure will not lead but rather will flow from the rest.

Sustaining your ministry is all about the long game and bringing people along with you!

Sustaining your ministry is all about the long game.

Q17 Planning Page

Ensure Long-Term Success

Please see pages 86–89, "Instructions for Question Planning Pages," for how to fill this out.

Suggested Tasks		
CRAWL	**Senior pastor coordination:** *Schedule a quarterly meeting with your senior pastor, sharing stats and stories to make sure you are both on the same page.*	
WALK	**Ministry alignment:** *List your various small group activities and programs, and evaluate with your C Team what is and isn't aligned to bring health and balance through groups. What course corrections are needed? Do you need to better communicate your system for health to church people?*	
RUN	**Renewal:** *Identify the current level of renewal for you, your small group ministry, and your church, and set a goal to begin the next level.*	

Your Dream	Obstacles	Actions	Timing
Long-Range (1–5 years)			
Short-Range (1–12 months)			
	Other Actions		

After you've completed this page, mark the highest-priority action for this planning question. Copy that action onto the prioritizing list, pages 221–23 in chapter 10.

How Will You Celebrate Stories of Life Change to Reach Your Vision?

Q18

Another important part of the sustaining phase is celebrating and learning from the life journeys of the people in your small groups. The Bible says, "Since we are receiving a Kingdom that is unshakable, let us be thankful and please God by worshiping him with holy fear and awe" (Heb. 12:28 NLT). Absorb that for a minute. *An unshakable kingdom.* If we have any cause for celebration, that is it. Make time throughout your small groups to worship God by celebrating what he is doing. You and others can share stories and life lessons powerfully through written and spoken word.

Stories are powerful motivators. Jesus was a master of using stories. Be creative in using stories to help small group leaders and members parlay your vision into action.

In Groups

Our regular celebration of what God is doing helps keep group leaders and members excited about the ministry and their part in it. We're all motivated by true stories about the supernatural God of this universe intersecting with our lives. When he demonstrates his infinite power and love, all we can say is, *Wow! Just wow, God!*

First remind leaders and members to stay aware, noticing what God is doing around them. If he isn't doing anything, they need to pray in confidence that he will amaze us. Encourage groups to write down their requests and God's responses.

Then when God responds, ask them to share the stories in their groups and, through the leaders, with you or your team. One great way to do this is making a group video (using someone's phone) to tell the story. Highlight the most relevant members as the stars, but also draw in the rest of the group and their thoughts. Ask leaders to send these videos to you or a designated assistant, who can evaluate them and edit for quality. Then post the videos to social media and your website, or catalog them for use by teaching pastors and as testimonies in services.

Stories of God's intervention in groups and individual lives will take your ministry to a new level. Guaranteed.

You can also request stories from specific group members and leaders. Guide their mental processing about the ways small group involvement has impacted their lives. What has caused them to follow Christ in new ways? What brought about changes in attitude and behavior?

I recommend you establish a system for gathering and archiving stories. You may hear a powerful testimony that you don't need now, but you may need it in a month or a year.

Continual Learning

I've successfully used the "Four Ps of Continual Learning" as a guide for sharing in groups, and it often draws out stories about God's unshakable kingdom in our lives. You may have seen the Four Ps in my previous books, and I've recently added a fifth. This is a tool you can pass along to your small group leaders and members to help them share their stories with each other.

What Is a Praise?

Something good is always going on. We find it easy and natural to complain about what's going wrong, but God wants us to see the glass half full. In small groups, share with each other what's going right, or what good is coming out of our circumstances—even our difficulties.

What Is a Problem?

Encourage group leaders and members to view and share problems as opportunities to learn. I guarantee that every problem is something someone else has encountered—possibly someone in the same group, possibly someone we can learn about in the Bible. Encourage your people to look around; they may connect with someone who has the solution or life lessons to draw from the problem.

What Is the Plan?

When your leaders and members share with each other about their hopes, they have greater experience and wisdom together to come up with plans for achieving those hopes. At Saddleback we guide small groups to work on balanced fulfillment of Jesus's Great Commission and great commandment in each other's lives. Some people's stories will illustrate ways this has happened in their past. These encourage others to write and live God's stories for their future.

What Is a Personal Prayer Request?

Group members can invite each other's prayers, asking our Father to help us live well the next step of our stories. We can also pray for each other's friends and family, as well as spiritual leaders, government officials, and more.

What Is Healthy Perspective?

Pray for and look for God's perspective on your life and your group experience. He has revealed much about his perspective through Scripture. When we rise above our usual limited horizons and gain his viewpoint, we find new reason to celebrate what he is doing and how our life and group circumstances are achieving his great plan. Our stories are all part of God's greater Story. Our lives are the global, history-spanning telling of his Story.

Q18 Planning Page

Celebrate Stories of Life Change

Please see pages 86–89, "Instructions for Question Planning Pages," for how to fill this out.

Suggested Tasks		
CRAWL	**Pray:** *Go to the prayer team you've recruited and ask them to pray regularly for life change to happen in your church's small groups so there will be stories to tell.*
WALK	**Share:** *In your small groups, encourage regular sharing of praises to honor what God has done in members' lives.*
RUN	**Proclaim:** *In services, schedule regular sharing of life-change testimonies about "God moments" in the lives of small group members.*

Your Dream	Obstacles	Actions	Timing
Long-Range (1–5 years)			
Short-Range (1–12 months)			
	Other Actions		

After you've completed this page, mark the highest-priority action for this planning question. Copy that action onto the prioritizing list, pages 221–23 in chapter 10.

How Will You Remain True to Your Call?

As you do everything it takes to sustain and grow your small group ministry, don't get so caught up in the tasks that you forget your calling.

After his resurrection, Jesus asked Peter, "Simon son of John, do you love me more than these?" (John 21:15). Three times Jesus asked, and three times Peter answered yes. What does Jesus mean by "these"? I think he was talking about 153 fish the disciples had just caught, on which they had just breakfasted. This may seem inconsequential, but every detail in Scripture is meaningful. For a first-century fisherman, a catch of 153 fish was striking the mother lode. It was a great boost for the livelihood of Peter and his family. Jesus wanted Peter to remember his calling, that Peter had initially trusted Jesus enough to leave "these" and follow him.

Before any of us can lead a ministry, we must be able to answer Jesus's question: "Do you love me more than these?" What does "these" mean to you? For me, it is security. Insecurity almost kept me from getting into ministry. Insecurity kills faith! For Peter it was livelihood. Peter ultimately wrestled down this temptation and willingly kept following Jesus as his highest life priority. The next time we see Peter, three thousand people are saved through his preaching!

If you are going to fulfill God's purpose for you in your church and your small group ministry, you can't forget your calling. Your ministry's long-term success is made more likely by your own longevity in your church overseeing that ministry. The longer you are able to share and enact your vision, the better your chances for permanently changing your church culture.

But if you are weary or overburdened, or even slightly unsettled, that may make it difficult for you to feed Jesus's sheep (see John 21:15–17). The devil works in sneaky ways. If he can't cause you to sin, he will do his best to keep you busy and distracted. Don't become so consumed with a checklist that you forget the real economy of your church and ministry: *people*! Keep your guardrails in place, balancing processes and people. Capitalize on prayer partners and mentors. Don't drift from your priorities,

Don't get so caught up in the tasks that you forget your calling.

including your priorities outside your ministry—your family, for example. God has given you a mission, and he will help you complete it!

It is imperative that you take care of your own soul. If you have trouble justifying the pursuit of biblical rest and restoration, you need no more excuse than the fact that your kingdom assignment depends on it. If you burn out, your ministry may burn out as well. If you aren't caring for your soul, you are more prone to becoming sidetracked.

Daniel Thomas at Highlands Fellowship Church in Abingdon, Virginia, wrote me a note about this very issue:

> My personality isn't one where I can simply turn off work mode. I found myself becoming frustrated and even exhausted with "the ministry." When I attended your conference, you challenged me to consider soul care and being true to my call to serve the local church. If I don't plan to stay true to my call, I can't be effective in serving others. Not only will I suffer, but so will those God has entrusted to my care. As will the evangelism that my small groups are doing.
>
> So I've developed a simple plan:
>
> 1. Schedule daily time with God in my calendar—This feeds my soul, and brings success in my ministry, because everything I do stems from my personal relationship with God.
> 2. Connect with a mentor regularly—When my mentor knows my plan, he or she can help me stay on track.
> 3. Connect with other small group point people or pastors either online or in person once a quarter (through the Small Group Network)—I love learning from others with ministry experience, as well as gaining fresh insight from those who are new. This also helps renew my passion.
> 4. Invest in others, share with someone what God is sharing with me—I believe God only gives to us as we pour ourselves into others.

In all the areas of growth and faithfulness you teach in your ministry—time with God, giving, fellowship with other Christians, and so on—you must see to these in your own life. Otherwise your ministry effectiveness will erode. The Casting Crowns song "Slow Fade" talks about how we can slide backward by small degrees. Nobody digs a spiritual hole with a backhoe, but typically one teaspoon at a time.

Of course all of the leaders in your ministry should be doing the same in order to ensure their effectiveness in their roles. But they are following your lead, so I'm purposefully directing this question toward you personally. Daily renew your passion rather than allowing your ministry to become a drudgery or burden. God wants your service to manifest the gifts he has given you, to win and draw people close to his Son, Jesus. What renews your soul? As the shepherd goes, so go the sheep.

As the shepherd goes, so go the sheep.

213

Q19 Planning Page

Remain True to Your Call

Please see pages 86–89, "Instructions for Question Planning Pages," for how to fill this out.

Suggested Tasks		
CRAWL	**Absolute surrender:** *List what God wants you to surrender. We all have an Achilles' heel. What will bring you, the point person for small groups, closer to God, which will in turn help you achieve his cause?*
WALK	**Keep him first:** *What are your "these" that you may love more than Jesus? Share this with a close friend who will pray for you.*
RUN	**Stay focused:** *List how many hours you give as the small group point person. Record your hours to see how much you are passively reacting and how much you are proactively pursuing priorities.*

Your Dream	Obstacles	Actions	Timing
Long-Range (1–5 years)			
Short-Range (1–12 months)			
	Other Actions		

After you've completed this page, mark the highest-priority action for this planning question. Copy that action onto the prioritizing list, pages 221–23 in chapter 10.

How Will You Help Your Groups Cultivate an Attitude of Worshipful Submission?

For this question I want to expand on the traditional definition of *worship*. Here it means complete submission to the Holy Spirit, total surrender, including sacrifice of the junk that is in us. The small group point person is the starting point for worshipful submission throughout the ministry. Our example trickles down through our leadership, so our personal submission and surrender to the Lord is a critical factor to everyone we lead. We must continually put ourselves on the altar as living sacrifices (see Rom. 12:1), knowing that God wields the knife as a surgeon, not an assassin. The following habits have kept me going for thirty-five years in ministry:

- *Quiet time*. Whatever it takes, I make it happen. I am a terrible reader, so I use audio via the Drivetime Devotions app. Ten minutes of Scripture sets the table for me to reflect with the Lord. Spend time with God to be used by him.
- *Tithing and time*. When God owns your finances, he owns you. When God owns your calendar, he owns you. Giving is worship.
- *Community*. Authentic human relationships—especially with those who love you in ways that improve you—make you more Christlike.

Worship helps you and your leaders connect the ministry dots so everyone "gets it." Helping all your leadership connect with God will do more than a hundred times as much as training. So in sustaining your ministry, keep yourself and your leaders in close touch with your best advocate, the Holy Spirit. The Holy Spirit held first-century churches together throughout all the chaos and turmoil, and he will do the same for yours. You may think you control your ministry, but it is his ministry, and he controls it. Plan for and expect meaningful experiences that allow God to do what only he can do, and it will make your job a lot easier!

At Saddleback we emphasize worship largely in three contexts within our small group ministry.

215

In Small Groups

Train your leaders to plan small group worship with care so it doesn't seem like a waste of time but rather an integral part of group members' spiritual health. When God commanded us to observe a Sabbath as part of submissive worship, he certainly didn't consider that a waste of time. We fear that taking a day off from work will put us behind. But God can do more with six days than we can do with seven. All other time devoted purely to God is equally meaningful and will renew us in ways we never thought possible. I myself struggle to believe this. But if I worked and rested my way, instead of God's way, I'd trash my marriage, my kids, even my ministry.

We encourage small groups to enjoy worship in numerous ways, both in group meetings and in members' lives seven days per week. Some groups may celebrate the Lord's Supper, delving deep into related Scriptures and prayer, so that members aren't limited to the brief experience in weekend services. Some groups also use:

- *Scripture meditation.* Someone reads a Scripture passage, then members silently dwell on the meaning and application of the teaching before sharing how it spoke to them.
- *Video.* The large selection of worship on video provides many options to play before or in response to Bible study.
- *Singing.* If your group has the talent, go for it. (If my small group sang, that would be our last meeting and the video would go viral!)
- *Communion.* This is powerful if your church polity allows it.

The ideas are countless. These are just suggestions to get the ball rolling.[1]

In Community Huddles

In some of our Community Huddles we gather a cluster of small group leaders (though anyone is welcome, and sometimes whole groups attend), not just to meet with each other, but also to meet with God. Sometimes God shows up in cool and varied ways. We may structure a Community Huddle this way:

- 30 percent training on God's Word and leading small groups
- 40 percent role-play related to the training, creating real or simulated experiences for people (as when our leaders recently practiced anointing with oil during training)
- 30 percent personal and heart, guiding leaders in meaningful corporate worship

In Leader Gatherings

As I've described earlier, we offer our Leader Gatherings twice per year, once to express appreciation, cast vision, and recruit, and another time for a night of worship. We keep it simple but effective. Not only do leaders enjoy a time of meaningful worship, but they also learn ways of leading their small groups in worship.

Q20 Planning Page

Cultivate an Attitude of Worshipful Submission

Please see pages 86–89, "Instructions for Question Planning Pages," for how to fill this out.

Suggested Tasks		
CRAWL	**Weekly:** *Invite small group members to take turns bringing their favorite worship videos for group worship, followed by reflection and sharing.*
WALK	**Quarterly:** *Encourage groups to plan special worship events, perhaps for communion, foot washing, nailing sins to a cross, extended prayer time, and other creative ideas.*
RUN	**Gatherings:** *Plan a night of worship to bring groups together for corporate worship, with or without a sermon, primarily to reflect on God.*

Your Dream	Obstacles	Actions	Timing
Long-Range (1–5 years)			
Short-Range (1–12 months)			
	Other Actions		

After you've completed this page, mark the highest-priority action for this planning question. Copy that action onto the prioritizing list, pages 221–23 in chapter 10.

PART 3

Conclusion

10

Putting It All Together

Congratulations! You are sooooo close to the end. Now that you have walked through the twenty questions, dreamed *big*, and brainstormed some smart goals for your small group ministry, you have accomplished what less than 3 percent of people in ministry have done. You are in the 97th percentile. I'm proud of your persistence and hard work. Now, what's next?

Prioritizing List

	ABC	123
Q1 How Will You Align Your Ministry with Other Church Leadership and Ministries?		
High-Priority Goal for **Q1**: _____		
Q2 How Will You Communicate the Value of Groups to Your Church?		
High-Priority Goal for **Q2**: _____		
Q3 What Is Your Plan for Connecting People into Groups?		
High-Priority Goal for **Q3**: _____		

ABC 123

Q4 How Will You Measure Your Progress?

High-Priority Goal for **Q4:** _____

_____

Q5 How Will You Define and Develop Mature Disciples?

High-Priority Goal for **Q5:** _____

_____

Q6 What Outcomes Do You Want from Small Group Life?

High-Priority Goal for **Q6:** _____

_____

Q7 How Will You Develop Leaders for Your Ministry?

High-Priority Goal for **Q7:** _____

_____

Q8 What Support Resources Will Your Small Group Leaders Need?

High-Priority Goal for **Q8:** _____

_____

Q9 How Will You Develop Group Members into Leaders?

High-Priority Goal for **Q9:** _____

_____

Q10 How Will Subgrouping Develop People?

High-Priority Goal for **Q10:** _____

_____

Q11 How Will You Encourage People to Serve?

High-Priority Goal for **Q11:** _____

_____

Q12 How Will You Create Opportunities for Groups to Serve?

High-Priority Goal for **Q12:** _____

_____

ABC 123

Q13 How Will You Promote Reach and Spiritual Awareness?

High-Priority Goal for **Q13**: _____

_____

Q14 How Will You Engage Every Group in Global Outreach?

High-Priority Goal for **Q14**: _____

_____

Q15 How Will You Engage Every Group in Local Outreach?

High-Priority Goal for **Q15**: _____

_____

Q16 How Will You Involve Every Group in Personal Evangelism?

High-Priority Goal for **Q16**: _____

_____

Q17 How Will You Ensure Your Ministry's Long-Term Success?

High-Priority Goal for **Q17**: _____

_____

Q18 How Will You Celebrate Stories of Life Change to Reach Your Vision?

High-Priority Goal for **Q18**: _____

_____

Q19 How Will You Remain True to Your Call?

High-Priority Goal for **Q19**: _____

_____

Q20 How Will You Help Your Groups Cultivate an Attitude of Worshipful Submission?

High-Priority Goal for **Q20**: _____

_____

Prioritize

Look at the prioritizing list of all twenty planning questions along with the twenty high-priority goals you chose as you worked through the book (pages 221–23). It's time to rank the twenty goals you've chosen. We will do this in three stages.

First, read through the twenty high-priority goals you've written. You will see two columns of empty boxes beside each goal. In the first column write A, B, or C to identify that goal's degree of *importance* or *ministry impact*.

A = Great importance or impact on our small group ministry

B = Moderate importance or impact on our small group ministry

C = Low importance or impact on our small group ministry

Say a quick prayer, and go do that now. Then come back and read the next instructions.

Welcome back. Second, in the second column add a numerical value within each A, B, and C grouping to identify which should be done first, second, third, and so on. In other words, consider the goals you marked with an A and assign numbers based on the order in which they should be done. So your A1 goal is the one you will do first; you will do your A2 goal second, and so on.

Then do the same for your B-level goals, marking them B1, B2, and so on. And finally, your C-level goals, in the order in which you want to accomplish them.

Do that now and then read the instructions that follow.

Third, after you've labeled all twenty goals with a letter and a number, pick five to seven goals that you would like to accomplish over the next twelve to eighteen months. Some goals will be challenging, some easier. This is where you have a chance to exercise daring faith. So while you certainly should exercise some reason, invite God's wisdom in stretching your expectations.

Don't assume you should do all of your A-level goals first and your C-level goals last. You may find that some "less important" tasks have to be done before you can start on others. Your church calendar may dictate what can and can't happen in the next months or year. And some changes may be too much too soon for your church or ministry culture. In fact, knocking out a few of the easier goals quickly gives you and your ministry reason for celebration. And some small steps end up paying off big over time.

To illustrate, I once had some B-level goals regarding singles' groups that I set aside as less important. I was busy working away on some of our more urgent plans, but Rick preached a sermon series that logically led to launching new singles' groups. I didn't think we could attempt those goals at that time, but God opened the door! The church culture at that time contributed to the easy execution of those goals.

Write below the top five to seven goals that you want to pursue during the next twelve to eighteen months.

Put Them on the Calendar

Now put your top five to seven goals, some of them in steps or stages, on your calendar. Some or all of this may require coordination with your top ministry leaders and other church leaders if you haven't already been coordinating with them throughout the whole process. Putting something on a calendar makes it suddenly more real and more urgent. This builds faith and helps you maintain your focus and stick to your priorities.

Calendars are living documents, and erasers and delete keys exist for a reason. Some dates may "float," depending on what else is going on in your church and ministry. If you suffer unavoidable delays, remember that God's delays are not God's denials.

Once you've written your goals on the calendar, now begins the work of making them happen. If it was easy, everyone would do it!

Timing may seem a simple concept, but the two New Testament words for "time" help us see a need for balance in our thinking. The Greek *chronos* (from which we derive "chronological" and "anachronism") refers to measurable clock time—seconds, minutes, hours, years. In contrast, the Greek *kairos* means "opportunity," "season," or "fitting time." A sequence of moments is *chronos*, emphasizing the duration of time; an appointed time is *kairos*, with no regard for duration. *Chronos* is linear and quantitative, while *kairos* is nonlinear and qualitative.

God's delays are not God's denials.

Your time-related planning requires both kinds of thinking in balance. But since each individual and church culture tends to lean toward one or the other, we have to work at keeping both in force. Those who like *chronos* want to stay on schedule, sticking strictly to plan, doing things right. We need this thinking to avoid drift from a good plan. Those drawn to *kairos* are more flexible, willing to sacrifice the "perfect" schedule if it means accomplishing something truly important, though possibly inconvenient. We need this thinking to evaluate the original plan and consider important changes to it.

These aspects of time relate to other aspects of life and ministry. Do you and your church tend to focus on doing things right or on doing the right things? Remember, both are important, and imbalance between the two leads to poor ministry health. For greatest eternal impact, assess the tendency for you, your ministry, and your church culture. Then work together to press back the other way as needed. This is why ministry is more an art than a science.

Strength for the Weak, Wisdom for the Foolish

If the task ahead of you seems overwhelming or you feel inadequate, let me tell you a little of what God has done in and through me. If I can do it, so can you!

I have a mild form of dyslexia, so when I read, I sometimes swap words or characters around, then I try to make sense as I go. In math I would work hard and solve a problem correctly, but I would invert a couple numbers and write down the wrong answer. I'll never forget my sixth grade teacher becoming frustrated that I never spelled my name completely—"Stev" instead of "Steve," or "Glade" instead of "Gladen." She often asked, "How will you make it if you can't spell your name?"

God called me into ministry, and I was sure he had the wrong person. (Later, when I was a youth pastor, kids used to tease me, saying I read from my own version of the Bible.) I ran from ministry for seven years. But much like Jonah, I couldn't outrun God.

During my master's program at Fuller Seminary, a guidance counselor told me I couldn't get my degree until I actually worked in a church. Novel concept, huh? I was totally happy in my secular job, but God had other plans. I was so scared. But God spoke to me through 1 Corinthians 2:4–5, where Paul said he didn't come with wise and persuasive words, but with the spirit of God's power. Boom!

When Jesus chose the Twelve, he didn't pick the most influential or the wealthiest or the elite. *He picked the most obedient*, and he worked with them. He will do the same with you, and *you will make a difference*.

Everyone experiences seasons of discouragement, and everyone has his or her critics. That's normal. You need to deal with it as realistically as you can, but don't focus on the negative. Keep refreshing your spirit to avoid burnout. Then get on with your good, Spirit-guided work of accomplishing your church's and ministry's vision and mission.

Never forget: *You are not alone.*

We're All in This Together

God has placed around you many people and organizations that are there to help and support you. Look around your own community and your church. Pray and watch for connections with the people who are there for you and you for them. And beyond your local circles, you can lean on the powerhouse of small group point people who are standing beside you in the Small Group Network (see chapter 6, Q8).

Shila Garrett, from Christ Fellowship, West Palm Beach, Florida, shared in a note,

> The Small Group Network provides a landscape where those who design biblical community can collaborate. As we share our individual, unique blueprints with those who are laboring alongside us, we benefit from their collective years of knowledge and experience. This environment refreshes me and preserves my creativity, perspective, and endurance in ministry.

Use the knowledge and support of those around you. This is a long game; press on and you will be successful. I love what author and speaker John C. Maxwell said:

> If it weren't for the leaders God placed in my life, I would not be able to invest in the lives of leaders around the world the way I do today. I cannot stress the importance of learning from other leaders for your life and your ministry. Saddleback's Small Group Network creates the ideal opportunity for you, as a leader in small group ministry, to grow and make a greater impact than you would have if you had tried to go at it alone.

Go make a difference. And if I can help further, you can always reach me at steve@stevegladen.com.

God bless!

Saddleback Church's Curriculum Pathway

For gap weeks use our sermon discussion guide "Talk It Over" at www .saddleback.com/talkitover.

Year One	Length	Category	Purpose
God's Design for Your Life	6 Weeks	Group Growth	All
God's Design for Great Relationships	4 Weeks	Group Growth	Fellowship
God's Design for Growing Spiritually	4 Weeks	Group Growth	Discipleship
God's Design for Greatness	4 Weeks	Group Growth	Ministry
God's Design for Changing the World	4 Weeks	Group Growth	Evangelism
God's Design for Worship	4 Weeks	Group Growth	Worship
What on Earth Am I Here For?	6 Weeks	Life Skills	All
Foundations—Intro to the Bible	4 Weeks	Doctrine	Discipleship
Annual Campaign	6 Weeks	Varies	Varies
	42 Weeks		

Year Two	Length	Category	Purpose
40 Days in the Word	6 Weeks	Spiritual Growth	Discipleship
Ephesians Chapter 1	4 Weeks	Bible	Discipleship
Foundations—God	4 Weeks	Doctrine	Discipleship
The Way of the Worshiper	4 Weeks	Spiritual Growth	Worship
Just Walk Across the Room	4 Weeks	Spiritual Growth	Evangelism
Christians in the Workplace	6 Weeks	Life Skills	All
Daniel Plan	6 Weeks	Life Skills	All
Annual Campaign	6 Weeks	Varies	Varies
	40 Weeks		

Year Three	Length	Category	Purpose
Sermon on the Mount, Part 1	6 Weeks	Spiritual Growth	Fellowship
Romans Chapter 8	4 Weeks	Bible	Discipleship
Foundations—Jesus	4 Weeks	Doctrine	Discipleship
Finding God in the Desert of the Soul	4 Weeks	Spiritual Growth	Worship
Foundations—Holy Spirit	4 Weeks	Doctrine	Discipleship
SHAPE	6 Weeks	Spiritual Growth	Ministry
40 Days of Community	6 Weeks	Life Skills	Fellowship
Annual Campaign	6 Weeks	Varies	Varies
	40 Weeks		

Year Four	Length	Category	Purpose
Sermon on the Mount, Part 2	6 Weeks	Spiritual Growth	Discipleship
1 Thessalonians, Part 1	6 Weeks	Bible	Discipleship
Foundations—Creation	4 Weeks	Doctrine	Discipleship
Choose Joy	4 Weeks	Spiritual Growth	Worship
The Passion	3 Weeks	Spiritual Growth	Evangelism
Developing Your Shape to Serve Others	6 Weeks	Spiritual Growth	Ministry
40 Days of Love	6 Weeks	Life Skills	Fellowship
Annual Campaign	6 Weeks	Varies	Varies
	41 Weeks		

Year Five	Length	Category	Purpose
Sermon on the Mount, Part 3	6 Weeks	Spiritual Growth	Ministry
1 Thessalonians, Part 2	6 Weeks	Bible	Discipleship
Foundations—Salvation	4 Weeks	Doctrine	Discipleship
Financial Fitness	5 Weeks	Life Skills	Worship
Wide Angle	6 Weeks	Spiritual Growth	Discipleship

Life Skills (choose one of the three)

	Length	Category	Purpose
God's Answers to Life's Difficult Questions	6 Weeks	Life Skills	Discipleship
Love-Powered Parenting	6 Weeks	Life Skills	Fellowship
Sacred Marriage	6 Weeks	Life Skills	Fellowship
Annual Campaign	6 Weeks	Varies	Varies
	39 Weeks		

Notes

Introduction

1. This is a variation on a quote attributed to Henry Ford ("Vision without execution is just hallucination") and Thomas Edison ("Vision without execution is hallucination"), as well as a Japanese proverb ("Vision without action is a daydream; action without vision is a nightmare").

2. Steve Gladen, *Small Groups with Purpose* (Grand Rapids: Baker, 2012), available at www.SmallGroups.net/store.

3. Thom S. Rainer, "Eight Major Changes in Churches the Past Ten Years," *Growing Healthy Churches Together*, May 10, 2017, www.thomrainer.com/2017/05/eight-major-changes-in-churches-the-past-ten-years.

Chapter 1 Think Churchwide

1. Rick Warren, *The Purpose Driven Church* (Grand Rapids: Zondervan, 1995), 103.

2. Warren, *Purpose Driven Church*, 146.

Chapter 3 Lead Effectively

1. Inspired by Doug Fields, *Your First Two Years in Youth Ministry: A Personal and Practical Guide to Starting Right* (Grand Rapids: Zondervan, 2002), 37–38.

Chapter 5 The Kitchen

1. See also Steve's podcast, "7 Ways to Lead Effective Small Group Ministry When Your Pastor May Not Be on Board," www.blog.SmallGroupNetwork.com/pastorbuyin.

2. Cade Metz, "Mark Zuckerberg's Answer to a World Divided by Facebook Is More Facebook," *Wired Business*, February 16, 2017, www.wired.com/2017/02/mark-zuckerbergs-answer-world-divided-facebook-facebook.

3. "Calculating Migration Expectancy Using ACS Data," United States Census Bureau, accessed January 16, 2018, https://www.census.gov/topics/population/migration/guidance/calculating-migration-expectancy.html.

4. Gretchen Livingston, "Fewer Than Half of U.S. Kids Today Live in a 'Traditional' Family," Pew Research Center, December 22, 2014, http://www.pewresearch.org/fact-tank/2014/12/22/less-than-half-of-u-s-kids-today-live-in-a-traditional-family.

5. Steve Gladen, *Leading Small Groups with Purpose* (Grand Rapids: Baker, 2012), available at www.SmallGroups.net/store.

Chapter 9 The Dining Room

1. I list over a hundred worship ideas for small groups in my books *250 Big Ideas for Small Group Leaders* and *Leading Small Groups with Purpose*, both available at www.SmallGroups.net/store.

Steve Gladen (MDiv, Fuller Theological Seminary) has been pastor of small groups at Saddleback Church since 1998 and serves as an elder of the church. He oversees the strategic launch and spiritual development of more than seven thousand adult small groups on multiple campuses. He is the author of *Small Groups with Purpose*, which has been translated into eleven languages to date, and *Leading Small Groups with Purpose*. He has a driving passion to see each church attendee connected to a qualified shepherd and become an integral part of the church body, living purposefully for Christ. Steve and his wife, Lisa, have been married for nearly thirty years and have two children, Erika and Ethan. They reside in Orange County, California. Learn more at www.stevegladen.com.

HOW TO **GROW** YOUR CHURCH'S
SMALL GROUP MINISTRY

This practical book walks you through the questions you need to answer to develop your own intentional small group strategy. Because it is built on principles and not methods, this step-by-step process can be implemented successfully in any size church.

BakerBooks

a division of Baker Publishing Group
www.BakerBooks.com

Available wherever books and ebooks are sold.

TAKE YOUR SMALL GROUP
TO THE NEXT LEVEL

For the new small group leader, the seasoned leader who feels their small group lacks purpose, or the leader who is itching to move their small group to the next level, *Leading Small Groups with Purpose* is the road map to follow. Every chapter includes ideas that you can implement immediately, as well as ways to shape your small group over time.

The Small Group Network was created in 2006 so you would have other small group ministry leaders to encourage you, to bounce ideas off of, to get ideas from, and to help you do the work God has called you to.

Put this book to work
Tool #1

SGN

Put HUNDREDS
of **small group
ministry leaders**
on your team

Free newsletter,
free resources!

Join us at
www.smallgroupnetwork.com

At the small group ministries website, you'll find over 300 free downloadable resources and the top resources used at Saddleback to build your ministry, to train your leaders, and to build health in your small groups.

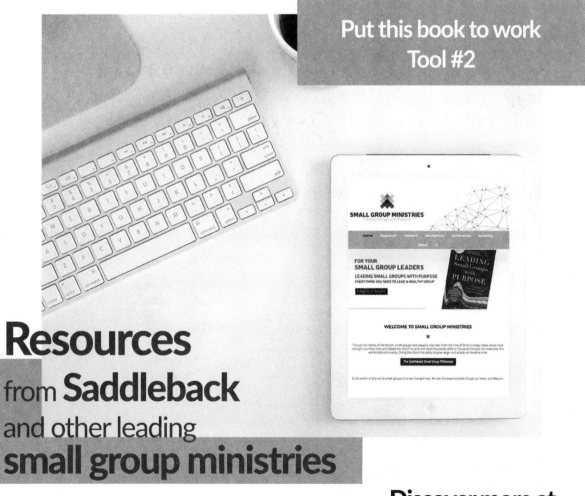

**Put this book to work
Tool #2**

Resources
from **Saddleback**
and other leading
small group ministries

Discover more at
www.smallgroups.net

SADDLEBACK CHURCH
INTERNSHIPS

Intern with Steve Gladen at Saddleback! We are a teaching and training church that's passionate about developing leaders wherever God is calling them. Our program is designed to provide a unique transformational learning and growth experience to each intern based on their ministry goals, interests, and passions.

Learn about the 50+ opportunities available for you to learn and lead at Saddleback!

Visit
saddleback.com/interns